First World War
and Army of Occupation
War Diary
France, Belgium and Germany

2 DIVISION
Divisional Troops
11 Sanitary Section
9 January 1915 - 30 March 1917

WO95/1339/2

The Naval & Military Press Ltd
www.nmarchive.com

Published in association with The National Archives

Published by

The Naval & Military Press Ltd

Unit 10 Ridgewood Industrial Park,

Uckfield, East Sussex,

TN22 5QE England

Tel: +44 (0) 1825 749494

www.naval-military-press.com

www.nmarchive.com

This diary has been reprinted in facsimile from the original. Any imperfections are inevitably reproduced and the quality may fall short of modern type and cartographic standards.

© **Crown Copyright**
Images reproduced by permission of The National Archives, London, England, 2015.

Contents

Document type	Place/Title	Date From	Date To
Heading	WO95/1339/2		
Heading	2nd Division No. II Sanitary Section Jan-Dec 1915		
Heading	No. II Sanitary Officer 2nd Division Vol I Jan 1915		
War Diary	Locon	09/01/1915	31/01/1915
Heading	No. II Sanitary Officer 2nd Division Vol II Feb 1915		
Heading	War Diary Of Sanitary Officer 2nd. Division February		
War Diary	Locon	01/02/1915	01/02/1915
War Diary	Bethune	02/02/1915	28/02/1915
Heading	No II Sanitary Officer 2nd. Division Vol III March 1915		
Heading	War Diary Sanitary Section 2nd. Division March 1915		
War Diary	Bethune	01/03/1915	20/03/1915
Miscellaneous	To The A.D.M.S. 2nd. Division Sanitary Report	21/03/1915	21/03/1915
Miscellaneous	To The A.D.M.S. 2nd. Division Sanitary Report	22/03/1915	22/03/1915
Miscellaneous	To A.D.M.S. 2nd Division	23/03/1915	23/03/1915
Miscellaneous	To The A.D.M.S. 2nd. Division	23/03/1915	23/03/1915
Miscellaneous	To The A.D.M.S. 2nd. Division	24/03/1915	24/03/1915
Miscellaneous	To A.D.M.S. 2nd. Division Sanitary Report		
Miscellaneous	To A.D.M.S. 2nd. Division Sanitary Report	26/03/1915	26/03/1915
Miscellaneous	To The A.D.M.S 2nd. Division Sanitary Report	27/03/1915	27/03/1915
Miscellaneous	To The A.D.M.S. 2nd Division Sanitary Report	28/03/1915	28/03/1915
War Diary		29/03/1915	31/03/1915
Heading	No. 11 Sanitary Officer 2nd Division Vol IV April 1915		
Heading	War Diary Of Sanitary Officer 22nd Division		
Miscellaneous	To A.D.M.S. 2nd. Div Report Of Sanitary Officer	01/04/1915	01/04/1915
Miscellaneous	A.D.M.S. 2nd. Div. Report Of Sanitary Officer	02/04/1915	02/04/1915
Miscellaneous	To A.D.M.S. 2nd. Division Report Of Sanitary Officer	03/04/1915	03/04/1915
Miscellaneous	To A.D.M.S. 2nd. Division Report Of Sanitary Officer	04/04/1915	04/04/1915
Miscellaneous	To A.D.M.S. 2nd. Division Report Of Sanitary Officer	05/04/1915	05/04/1915
Miscellaneous	To A.D.M.S. 2nd. Divn. Report Of Sanitary Officer	06/04/1915	06/04/1915
Miscellaneous	A.D.M.S. 2nd. Divn. Report Of Sanitary Officer	07/04/1915	07/04/1915
Miscellaneous	To A.D.M.S. 2nd. Div. Report Of Sanitary Officer	08/04/1915	08/04/1915
Miscellaneous	To A.D.M.S. 2nd. Division Report Of Sanitary Officer	09/04/1915	09/04/1915
Miscellaneous	To A.D.M.S. 2nd. Division Report Of Sanitary Officer	10/04/1915	10/04/1915
Miscellaneous	To A.D.M.S. 2nd. Division Report Of Sanitary Officer	11/04/1915	11/04/1915
Miscellaneous	To A.D.M.S. 2nd. Divn. Report Of Sanitary Officer	12/04/1915	12/04/1915
Miscellaneous	A.D.M.S. 2nd. Divn. Report Of Sanitary Officer	13/04/1915	13/04/1915
Miscellaneous	To A.D.M.S. 2nd. Division Report Of Sanitary Officer	14/04/1915	14/04/1915
Miscellaneous	A.D.M.S. 2nd. Divn. Report Of Sanitary Officer	30/04/1915	30/04/1915
Miscellaneous	A.D.M.S. 2nd. Divn. Report Of Sanitary Officer	15/04/1915	15/04/1915
Miscellaneous	A.D.M.S. 2nd. Divn. Report Of Sanitary Officer	16/04/1915	16/04/1915
Miscellaneous	To A.D.M.S. 2nd. Divn. Report Of Sanitary Officer	17/04/1915	17/04/1915
Miscellaneous	To A.D.M.S. 2nd. Divn. Report Of Sanitary Officer	18/04/1915	18/04/1915
Miscellaneous	To A.D.M.S. 2nd. Divn. Report Of Sanitary Officer	19/04/1915	19/04/1915
Miscellaneous	A.D.M.S. 2nd. Divn. Report Of Sanitary Officer	20/04/1915	20/04/1915
Miscellaneous	A.D.M.S. 2nd. Divn. Report Of Sanitary Officer	21/04/1915	21/04/1915
Miscellaneous	To A.D.M.S. 2nd. Division Report Of Sanitary Officer	22/04/1915	22/04/1915
Miscellaneous	A.D.M.S. 2nd. Divn. Report Of Sanitary Officer	23/04/1915	23/04/1915
Miscellaneous	A.D.M.S. 2nd. Divn. Report Of Sanitary Officer	24/04/1915	24/04/1915
Miscellaneous	A.D.M.S. 2nd. Divn. Report Of Sanitary Officer	25/04/1915	25/04/1915
Miscellaneous	A.D.M.S. 2nd. Divn. Report Of Sanitary Officer	26/04/1915	26/04/1915

Miscellaneous	A.D.M.S. 2nd. Divn. Report Of Sanitary Officer	27/04/1915	27/04/1915
Miscellaneous	A.D.M.S. 2nd. Divn. Report Of Sanitary Officer	28/04/1915	28/04/1915
Miscellaneous	A.D.M.S. 2nd. Divn. Report Of Sanitary Officer	29/04/1915	29/04/1915
Heading	No. 11 Sanitary Officer 2nd. Division15 Vol V May 1915		
Miscellaneous	A.D.M.S. 2nd. Divn. Report Of Sanitary Officers	03/05/1915	03/05/1915
Miscellaneous	A.D.M.S. 2nd. Divn. Report Of Sanitary Officers	04/05/1915	04/05/1915
Miscellaneous	A.D.M.S. 2nd. Divn. Report Of Sanitary Officers	05/05/1915	05/05/1915
Miscellaneous	A.D.M.S. 2nd. Divn. Report Of Sanitary Officers	06/05/1915	06/05/1915
Miscellaneous	A.D.M.S. 2nd. Divn. Report Of Sanitary Officers	07/05/1915	07/05/1915
Miscellaneous	A.D.M.S. 2nd. Divn. Report Of Sanitary Officers	08/05/1915	08/05/1915
Miscellaneous	A.D.M.S. 2nd. Divn. Report Of Sanitary Officers	09/05/1915	09/05/1915
Miscellaneous	A.D.M.S. 2nd. Divn. Report Of Sanitary Officers	10/05/1915	10/05/1915
Miscellaneous	A.D.M.S. 2nd. Divn. Report Of Sanitary Officers	11/05/1915	11/05/1915
Miscellaneous	A.D.M.S. 2nd. Divn. Report Of Sanitary Officers	12/05/1915	12/05/1915
Miscellaneous	A.D.M.S. 2nd. Divn. Report Of Sanitary Officers	13/05/1915	13/05/1915
Miscellaneous	A.D.M.S. 2nd. Divn. Report Of Sanitary Officers	14/05/1915	14/05/1915
Miscellaneous	A.D.M.S. 2nd. Divn. Report Of Sanitary Officers	15/05/1915	15/05/1915
Miscellaneous	A.D.M.S. 2nd. Divn. Report Of Sanitary Officers	23/05/1915	23/05/1915
Miscellaneous	A.D.M.S. 2nd. Divn. Report Of Sanitary Officer	24/05/1915	24/05/1915
Miscellaneous	A.D.M.S. 2nd Division Report of Sanitary Officers	25/05/1915	25/05/1915
Miscellaneous	A.D.M.S. 2nd. Divn. Report Of Sanitary Officers	28/05/1915	28/05/1915
Miscellaneous	A.D.M.S. 2nd. Divn. Report Of Sanitary Officers	16/05/1915	16/05/1915
Miscellaneous	A.D.M.S. 2nd. Divn. Report Of Sanitary Officers	17/05/1915	17/05/1915
Miscellaneous	A.D.M.S. 2nd. Divn. Report Of Sanitary Officers	18/05/1915	18/05/1915
Miscellaneous	A.D.M.S. 2nd. Divn. Report Of Sanitary Officers	19/05/1915	19/05/1915
Miscellaneous	A.D.M.S. 2nd. Divn. Report Of Sanitary Officers	20/05/1915	20/05/1915
Miscellaneous	A.D.M.S. 2nd. Divn. Report Of Sanitary Officers	21/05/1915	21/05/1915
Miscellaneous	A.D.M.S. 2nd. Divn. Report Of Sanitary Officer	22/05/1915	22/05/1915
Miscellaneous	A.D.M.S. 2nd. Divn. Report Of Sanitary Officer	29/05/1915	29/05/1915
Miscellaneous	A.D.M.S. 2nd. Divn. Report Of Sanitary Officers	31/05/1915	31/05/1915
Heading	No. 11 Sanitary Section 2nd. Division Vol VI June 1915		
Heading	War Diary O.C. Sanitary Section 2nd. Division June 1915		
Miscellaneous	A.D.M.S. 2nd. Divn. Report Of Sanitary Officers For Week	07/06/1915	07/06/1915
Miscellaneous	A.D.M.S. 2nd. Divn. Report Of Sanitary Officers	08/06/1915	08/06/1915
Miscellaneous	A.D.M.S. 2nd. Divn. Report Of Sanitary Officers	11/06/1915	11/06/1915
Miscellaneous	A.D.M.S. 2nd. Divn. Report Of Sanitary Officers	12/06/1915	12/06/1915
Miscellaneous	A.D.M.S. 2nd. Divn. Report Of Sanitary Officers	14/06/1915	14/06/1915
Miscellaneous	A.D.M.S. 2nd. Divn. Report Of Sanitary Officers	15/06/1915	15/06/1915
Miscellaneous	A.D.M.S. 2nd. Divn. Report Of Sanitary Officer	16/06/1915	16/06/1915
Miscellaneous	A.D.M.S. 2nd. Divn. Report Of Sanitary Officers	17/06/1915	17/06/1915
Miscellaneous	A.D.M.S. 2nd. Divn. Report Of Sanitary Officers	18/06/1915	18/06/1915
Miscellaneous	A.D.M.S. 2nd. Divn. Report Of Sanitary Officers	19/06/1915	19/06/1915
Miscellaneous	A.D.M.S. 2nd. Divn. Report Of Sanitary Officers	20/06/1915	20/06/1915
Miscellaneous	A.D.M.S. 2nd. Divn. Report Of Sanitary Officers	21/06/1915	21/06/1915
Miscellaneous	A.D.M.S. 2nd. Divn. Report Of Sanitary Officer	22/06/1915	22/06/1915
Miscellaneous	A.D.M.S. 2nd. Divn.	23/06/1915	23/06/1915
Miscellaneous	A.D.M.S. 2nd. Divn. Report Of Sanitary Officers	24/06/1915	24/06/1915
Miscellaneous	A.D.M.S. 2nd. Divn.	25/06/1915	25/06/1915
Miscellaneous	A.D.M.S. 2nd. Divn.	27/06/1915	27/06/1915
Miscellaneous	A.D.M.S. 2nd. Divn.	28/06/1915	28/06/1915
Miscellaneous	A.D.M.S. 2nd. Divn. Report Of Sanitary Officers	29/06/1915	29/06/1915
Miscellaneous	A.D.M.S. 2nd. Divn. Report Of Sanitary Officers	30/06/1915	30/06/1915

Heading	No. 11 Sanitary Section Vol VII July 1915		
Miscellaneous		31/07/1915	31/07/1915
Miscellaneous	A.D.M.S. 2nd. Divn. Sanitary Officers Report		
Miscellaneous	A.D.M.S. 2nd. Divn. Sanitary Officers Report	30/07/1915	30/07/1915
Miscellaneous		29/07/1915	29/07/1915
Miscellaneous	A.D.M.S. II Divn.		
Miscellaneous	A.D.M.S. II Divn. Report Of Sanitary Officers	28/07/1915	28/07/1915
Miscellaneous	A.D.M.S. II Divn. Report Of Sanitary Officers	27/07/1915	27/07/1915
Miscellaneous	A.D.M.S. 2nd. Divn. Report Of Sanitary Officers	26/07/1915	26/07/1915
Miscellaneous	A.D.M.S. 2nd. Divn. Report Of Sanitary Officers	24/07/1915	24/07/1915
Miscellaneous	A.D.M.S. 2nd. Divn. Report Of Sanitary Officers	23/07/1915	23/07/1915
Miscellaneous	A.D.M.S. 2nd. Divn. Report Of Sanitary Officers	21/07/1915	21/07/1915
Miscellaneous	A.D.M.S. 2nd. Divn. Report Of Sanitary Officers	20/07/1915	20/07/1915
Miscellaneous	A.D.M.S. 2nd. Divn. Report Of Sanitary Officers	18/07/1915	18/07/1915
Miscellaneous	A.D.M.S. 2nd. Divn. Report Of Sanitary Officers	17/07/1915	17/07/1915
Miscellaneous	A.D.M.S. 2nd. Divn. Report Of Sanitary Officers	16/07/1915	16/07/1915
Miscellaneous	A.D.M.S. 2nd. Divn. Report Of Sanitary Officers	14/07/1915	14/07/1915
Miscellaneous	A.D.M.S. 2nd. Divn. Report Of Sanitary Officers	13/07/1915	13/07/1915
Miscellaneous	A.D.M.S. 2nd. Divn. Report Of Sanitary Officers	12/07/1915	12/07/1915
Miscellaneous	A.D.M.S. 2nd. Divn. Report Of Sanitary Officers	10/07/1915	10/07/1915
Miscellaneous	A.D.M.S. 2nd. Divn. Report Of Sanitary Officers	09/07/1915	09/07/1915
Miscellaneous	A.D.M.S. 2nd. Divn. Report Of Sanitary Officers	08/07/1915	08/07/1915
Miscellaneous	A.D.M.S. 2nd. Divn. Report Of Sanitary Officers	07/07/1915	07/07/1915
Miscellaneous	A.D.M.S. 2nd. Divn. Report Of Sanitary Officers	06/07/1915	06/07/1915
Miscellaneous	A.D.M.S. 2nd. Divn. Report Of Sanitary Officers	05/07/1915	05/07/1915
Miscellaneous	A.D.M.S. 2nd. Divn. Report Of Sanitary Officers	04/07/1915	04/07/1915
Miscellaneous	A.D.M.S. 2nd. Divn. Report Of Sanitary Officers	01/07/1915	01/07/1915
Miscellaneous	A.D.M.S. 2nd. Divn. Report Of Sanitary Officers	02/07/1915	02/07/1915
Miscellaneous	A.D.M.S. 2nd. Divn. Report Of Sanitary Officers	03/07/1915	03/07/1915
Heading	2nd. Division Medical No. 11 Sanitary Section Jan-Dec 1916		
Heading	War Diary Of No. 11 Sanitary Section-2nd. Division For The Months Of January And February & March 1916		
Heading	War Diary No. 11 Sanitary Section 2nd. Division Vol I II III		
War Diary	Busnes	01/01/1916	29/03/1916
Miscellaneous	Summary Of Infection Diseases For First 3 Month Jan Feb March		
Heading	War Diary No. 11 Sanitary Section 2nd. Division For April May		
War Diary		09/04/1916	12/05/1916
Heading	No. 11 Sanitary Section April & May 1916		
War Diary		13/05/1916	31/05/1916
Heading	2nd Division No. 11 Sanitary Section June 1916		
War Diary		01/06/1916	03/06/1916
War Diary	Camblain L'Abbe	03/06/1916	30/06/1916
Heading	War Diary Of No. 11 Sanitary Section 2nd. Division For July 1916 Vol 22		
War Diary		01/07/1916	31/07/1916
Heading	2nd. Division No. 11 Sanitary Section Aug 1916		
Heading	War Diary No. 11 Sanitary Section 2nd. Div. To August 1916		
War Diary		01/08/1916	31/08/1916
Heading	2nd. Div. 11th. Sanitary Section Sept 1916		

Heading	War Diary No. 11 Sanitary Section 2nd. Div. For Month Of September 1916		
War Diary		01/09/1916	30/09/1916
Miscellaneous	Appendix 1 Standing Orders For The Foden Thresh Disinfector	22/09/1916	22/09/1916
Heading	2nd. Division 11th. Sanitary Section Oct 1916		
Heading	War Diary Of No. 11 Sanitary Section 2nd. Division For October 1916		
War Diary		01/10/1916	31/10/1916
Miscellaneous	Summary of Infection Diseases notified during October 1916		
Heading	11th. Div. No. 11 Sanitary Section Nov 1916		
War Diary		01/11/1916	30/11/1916
Miscellaneous	Summary Of Infection Diseases For The Month		
Heading	2nd. Divn. No. 11 Sanitary Section Dec 1916		
Heading	War Diary No. 11 Sanitary Section 2nd. Division For December 1916		
War Diary		01/12/1916	31/12/1916
Miscellaneous	Summary Of Infection During For December		
Heading	2 Div. 11 San Sect 1917-Jan-1917 March		
Heading	2nd. Division No. 11 Sanitary Section Jan 1917		
War Diary	Brailly	01/01/1917	09/01/1917
War Diary	Cramont	09/01/1917	31/01/1917
Heading	2nd. Divn. 11th. Sanitary Section Feb 1917		
Heading	War Diary Of No. 11 Sanitary Section For February 1917		
War Diary	Cramont	02/02/1917	04/02/1917
War Diary	Aveluy	04/02/1917	05/02/1917
War Diary	Bouzincourt	05/02/1917	20/02/1917
War Diary	Albert	20/02/1917	27/02/1917
Heading	2nd. Divn. No. 11 Sanitary Section March 1917		
War Diary	Albert	01/03/1917	30/03/1917
Miscellaneous	Of No. 11 Sanitary Section During The Month Of March		
Heading	2 Division Troops 100 Field Ambulance 1915 Nov To 1919 June 11 Sanitary Section 1915 Jan To 1917 Mar		

WO 95
1339/2

2ND DIVISION
MEDICAL

NO. 11 SANITARY SECTION
JAN - DEC 1915

Jan 1915

S

12/4527
Jan 1915

Summonsed but not called

No. 11. Sanitary Officer, 2nd Division

Vol I.

Date Time Place	Events	Remarks
Jan 9th 1915 LOCON	Left BETHUNE with No 11 Section 2nd London Sanitary Co to report to A.D.M.S. 2nd Division. Billeted men in single house in LOCON. In afternoon went with D.A.D.M.S. 2nd Divn to VIELLE CHAPELLE and RICHEBOURG ST VAAST to note sanitary condition of these places in Divisional Area.	Col Holt Major Irvine
Jan 10	Split Section up into 3 parties. 1st party remained to clean up billet & prepare an orderly room. 2nd party sent by lorry to VIELLE CHAPELLE to report for work to Capt Heslop; 3rd party sent by lorry to RICHEBOURG ST VAAST. Arranged with Brigade hqrs to drain filthy ditches in village. Fatigue party of 30 men and own parts of 4 set to work on this. Apparently very little civilian labour is available in this area.	
Jan 11	Sent out party of 1 NCO & 9 men	

Date Time Place	Events	Remarks
	to RICHEBOURG ST VAAST. Started pumping out, by means of pump obtained from R.E., the foul ditch in front of Brigade Headquarters. Left party of men to be billeted in village and commence cleaning up of empty billets & roads of refuse. Refuse to be burnt or buried. Remainder of section engaged on own billet in LOCON.	
Jan 12	Squad continued working in village of RICHEBOURG. Started incinerator for rubbish in LOCON and cleaned up parts of roads in LOCON.	
Jan 13	RICHEBOURG.— Saw Corporal in charge of work here. Cleaning up of empty billets gradually proceeding. Arranged for following civilian labour to start work:— RICHEBOURG ST VAAST — 10 men to start on Friday Jan 15th VIELLE CHAPELLE — 3 men and 16 boys been at work here for past week. LA COUTURE — 2 men and 5 boys to commence work Jan 12 & under direction of the Maire, to	

Date Time Place	Events	Remarks
	clear up refuse in village & burn it.	
	LOCON — arranged with the Maire for 20 men to start on Jan. 15th at Les Choquaux and at Zelobes.	
	ROBECQ — disinfected clothing of 4 clerks in measles case.	
Jan 14.	Paid 259 francs for one week's civilian labour in VIEILLE CHAPELLE. Withdrew sanitary squad from RICHEBOURG ST. VAAST and LA COUTURE owing to change in Divisional area, and set them to work clearing refuse from the districts of LE TOURET and RUE DE L'EPINETTE. 20 civilians will proceed from LOCON tomorrow to work on the area occupied by H.L.I at LES CHOQUAX. Arranged with Staff Captain 6th Inf. Brigade to see area at HINGES they will occupy.	

Date.	Events.	Remarks.
Jan 15.	Located 2 cases of measles notified by Maire of LOCON; position X 13 b and d on Map France (BETHUNE). In one farm a platoon of Royal Berks were billetted. Notified their M.O. and got men removed. Squad of 20 civilians (10 men, 10 boys) sent from LOCON at 8.30 am for work at LES CHOQUAX. In afternoon handed these over to M.O. Royal Berkshires for work under his direction to get his billetting area cleaned. This was area previously left by 9th H.L.I in very dirty state. 2 parties of sanitary section continued work at LE TOURET and RUE DE L'EPINETTE. Fetched Creosol and Chloride of Lime from railhead MERVILLE. No formalin could be got here.	
Jan 16.	Placed out of bounds for all troops the houses located yesterday with cases of measles. Work at LE TOURET, RUE DE	

Events

L'EPINETTE and LES CHOQUAUX
was continued.
Notified unofficially of case of
diptheria at LE TOURET and one of
measles at the same place, but
failed to locate them.
Carried out a thorough inspection
of billets occupied in LOCON area by
3rd Coldstream Guards and 114 Heavy
R.G.A. Found them in fair
sanitary condition. Some
rubbish along canal required clearing
up.

Jan 17. Located 2 cases of disease at
LE TOURET and placed houses
out of bounds.
In LOCON district Sanitary Squad
has cleaned up Headquarters of
R.A. and part of area occupied
by 3rd Coldstream Gds found
dirty yesterday.
Civilian Labour continued
at LES CHOQUAUX.
Fitted up rooms in empty
house in LOCON district for

Events

disinfection of verminous blankets of 1st Herts Battalion by Sulphur fumigation. Steam Steriliser on wheels would be much more rapid in action but one not obtained yet.

Jan 18. Snow all day. Roads and open yards in most billets very sloppy in consequence
Commenced Sulphur fumigation of blankets.
Started building an incinerator at HQ of R.A. Locon.
20 civilians from Locon worked on area at ESSARS.
Inspected some billets of 1st Worcesters at GORRE; arranged to send here tomorrow party from sanitary Section to superintend cleaning up of Worcester's area.

Jan 19. Sent party of men to GORRE to superintend work for 2nd Worcesters.
As nearly all available ground has been used for latrines I recommended

Events.

purchasing large pails and emptying
contents of these, after use, into a
pit.
ESSARS — 25 civilians finished
cleaning up this area.
LOCON — 250 Blankets disinfected
for 1st Herts Battalion
Destructor at H.Q. of R.A. completed

Jan 20.

LOCON. — continued disinfection
of Blankets by sulphur fumigation.
Paid 240.fr 25c for civil labour
from LOCON, and 4.9 francs for civil
labour from LA COUTURE.
Inspected Back of Headquarters 2nd
Division and found this in
most insanitary state. Asked
Camp Commandant for fatigue
party for work on this tomorrow.
Recommended system of night urine
tubs and pails for defaecation.

Jan 21.

LOCON. Disinfection of blankets
of 1st Herts completed. Wired for
800 more from 4th Brigade to
come tomorrow. Divisional

Events.

Headquarters were cleaned up by fatigue party and prisoners working under supervision of Sanitary Section. Started system of night urine tubs and pails.

Many ditches in LOCON have become waterlogged and insanitary. Party from Sanitary Section was started draining and cleaning them. This work will have to be continued for 2 or 3 days.

Bought in BETHUNE 16 large pails for use at GORRE and at Divisional Headquarters.

Jan 22.

LOCON. Fatigue party of prisoners continued cleaning up Divisional Headquarters.
Various ditches in the village cleaned out.
100 blankets of 1st Irish Guards disinfected. Fitted up a second room for Sulphur fumigation.
ESSARS. With M.O of 2nd Oxs & Bucks L.I. I inspected billet where case of cerebrospinal meningitis had

Events.

occurred. This was in a loft in an open barn and could not readily be disinfected by spraying with formalin. Men in this billet removed and isolated for observation.

FESTUBERT. Fatigue party of 30 men at work here under supervision of 2 men from Sanitary Section, engaged in burying dead animals and clearing out refuse from ruined houses.

Jan 23rd. LOCON. Work at Headquarters continued. Further work on dirty ditches was commenced.
RICHEBOURG L'AVOUÉ. Disinfected a billet where case of meningitis had occurred here.
~~RICHEBOURG L'AVOUÉ~~
FESTUBERT. Work continued as yesterday.

Jan 24. Men of Sanitary Section engaged on odd jobs in Locon. Found area occupied by Irish Guards to be dirty.

Date	Events
Jan 25.	LOCON. Work of prisoners continued at Headquarters 2nd Division and in the village.
State of area occupied by Scottish Guards reported to their M.O. who promised to get refuse cleaned up by fatigue party.
LES CHOQUAX. The billets here occupied by the 2nd Grenadier Gds. are fairly clean, except for this morning's refuse which the men had not time to clean up before being suddenly called out to GIVENCHY.
GORRE. 14 large buckets were handed over by me to the M.O. 2nd H.L.I. for latrine purposes. He arranged for these to be cleaned daily, and handed over to the relieving unit, on his leaving this area.

Two box (portable) steam Sterilisers arrived for Sanitary Section today, but no Thresh's Steriliser. |

Date	Events
Jan. 26. Locon	LOCON Arrangements made for the RAMC sanitary men attached to Divisional Headquarters to obtain prisoners when necessary for the work of keeping the place clean.

Men from Sanitary Section have been engaged in cleaning ditches in the neighbourhood.

Party of prisoners also sent out to work on BETHUNE - ZELOBES road.
One box steriliser has been fitted up in LOCON & is now ready for sterilising clothes etc.

FESTUBERT Fatigue party could not work here on account of village being shelled again. |
| Jan. 27. | With A.D.M.S. 2nd Divn. I visited today the areas CORNET MALO, LES CHOQUAUX and ESSARS. All billets in these areas were |

Date	Events

found satisfactory except the Estaminet de la BELLE VUE in LES CHOQUAUX, which has now been placed out of bounds, and the first farm on East side of road ESSARS to GORRE, in which there are at present about 70 men of the 2nd OXF & Bucks L.I. and some refugees. This latter place will also be put out of bounds if sufficient accommodation can be found for the men in another part of village.

The emptying of foul ditches in these villages would require an enormous amount of labour.

Parties from Sanitary Section were engaged in work at FESTUBERT, LE TOURET, ESSARS, and LOCON.

Paid 683 francs 20 centimes for civilian labour at LA COUTURE and LE TOURET from Jan 7th to 18th.

Date	Events

Jan 28.
Locon

Parties from Sanitary Section engaged in supervising fatigue parties at work at LE TOURET, ESSARS, 5th Inf. Brigade Headquarters at LOWNE, and at LOCON.

100 Blankets of 1st Irish Guards disinfected.
All men in No. 3. Coy, 1st Irish Gds. were questioned as to whether they had ever had enteric; report sent in by M.O. to the A.D.M.S. 2nd Division.
Sergeant Tyler reported fouling of ESSARS by 2nd & 3rd Coldstream Gds. today during a halt; report sent to the O.C. by A.D.M.S.

Jan 29.   ESSARS. This area has now been cleaned up and a considerable amount of water drained away from the ditches.
HINGES.   Chateau cleaned up by Sanitary Squad today.

Jan 30. Visited billets in HINGES just vacated by 1st Herts battalion; report as to their condition & if latrines sent by A.D.M.S. to the O.C.
Billet occupied by 2nd Signal Coy. R.E.

Date	Events
	on the main LOCON-BETHUNE road at HALTE was found dirty & immediately cleaned up by my orders. In afternoon I went with Capt. Bell, Sanitary Officer 1st Division, to see some of the principal billets in BÉTHUNE. A report by Capt. BELL is to be forwarded to A.D.M.S. 2nd Division.
Jan 31st LOCON	Went out with Sanitary Officer 1st Div. to ANNEQUIN in my new area to inspect billets. Sanitary Section at work locally

Enumerated but not copied

13/4/15
Feb 19.15

No 11 Sanitary Officer 2nd Division.

Vol II.

WAR DIARY
OF
Sanitary Officer
2nd Division
February.

Date	Events
Feb 1st LOCON.	Inspected 200 men of draft for 2nd Grenadier Guards for suspicious sore throats. They have been contacts of a case of meningitis at CHELSEA; left CHELSEA Jan 22nd. No suspicious cases found. Sanitary Section got ready to move to BETHUNE tomorrow.
Feb 2nd BETHUNE	Moved Sanitary Section into BETHUNE. Billetted them with No 6 Field Ambulance in Institution St. Vaast. I arranged with the Town Commandant (Colonel Master) for carts to start work this morning for removal of refuse from the principal billets in the town. Sent round men of Sanitary Section to inspect and report on these places.
Feb 3rd.	Case of diphtheria at ESSARS reported by M.O. 2nd Worcesters. I investigated this and found 1 child in cottage position X 190 had been sent in to hospital in BETHUNE. Soldiers'

Date.	Events

underclothing in the house was seized by me and sterilised by steam. Clothing returned to M.O. 2nd Worcesters. House placed out of bounds and notified same to H.Q. 2nd Divn.

Town of BETHUNE has been divided by me into four areas for sanitary inspection, and each area has been placed in the charge of a sanitary Inspector from our Sanitary section. He will have supervisory ~~charge~~ of all the latrines, washing & billetting arrangements of troops and will report to me daily. He will also see to the disposal of refuse by incinerators and by carts.

I have made arrangements thereby horses and drivers shall be drawn from the 2nd Divisional Train and carts obtained from civilians.

I visited today some of the principal big billets in the town e.g. the Tobacco factory, Orphanage, Ecole Michelet etc.

Date & Place	Events
Feb. 4 BETHUNE	H.Q. 2nd Division report that the large billets previously used by troops of 1st Divn. will not be used now except one for a battalion. The amount of refuse left behind by 1st Divn. troops in these places is sufficient to occupy 100 to 150 men for several days in clearing it away. I therefore sent a request to Major Bruud D.A.Q.M.G. 2nd Divn. for a fatigue party from 1st Divn. Prisoners obtained from Town Commandant & men of my own sanitary section have been employed in removing this refuse but a much larger number of men is required.
Feb. 5.	With A.D.M.S. I inspected most of the above billets. <u>TOBACCO FACTORY</u> — recently vacated by 1st Northants. & 4th Sussex Regts. Is in a very dirty condition ; an enormous accumulation of refuse and manure in yard at entrance. <u>ECOLE MICHELET</u> — vacated by Black Watch. Also in a very bad state.

Date.	Events

ECOLE DE JEUNES FILLES. — Recently vacated by 2nd Batt. Both Regt. A large accumulation of rubbish here. Rooms left quite clean.

In view of all this refuse which requires removing. I have asked for fatigue party of 150 men from 1st Div.

50 men of Black Watch returned this evening to clean up their billet tomorrow.

Feb 6
BETHUNE.

GORRE. Three cases of diphtheria reported by M.O. 9th H.L.I. Went out to investigate it. House isolated. Platoon No 7 No 2 Co. put in this house for isolation. Arranged for blankets to be sterilised, & also underclothing of that can be done. Full report of names of men, position of House etc sent in to A.D.M.S.

BETHUNE. ECOLE MICHELET now reported clean by my Sergeant.

Date	Events
	Part of this School is occupied by a detachment of the 1st Queen's Regt. Parties from Sanitary Section have been engaged on other billets in the town. I have reported several cases of accumulation of civilian refuse in the streets to the Maire who promised to do his best to have them removed.
Feb. 7	Inspected billet of Coldstream Guards in BÉTHUNE — the ORPHANAGE. Entrance Yard very dirty & large accumulation of rubbish. Have arranged for an ablution bench to be fixed up by private contract, & purchased 10 tin hand basins for that same. Field used for latrines in very muddy condition. I have therefore ordered its use to be discontinued & 12 buckets from Tobacco Factory provided instead. The Sleeping rooms are large, but some are overcrowded.

Date	Events
Feb. 8.	With 4 Sanitary Inspectors from Sanitary Section I went over most of the town of BETHUNE inspecting billets etc. Sent in reports to A.D.M.S. on i Physics & Chemistry College, PLACE DE LILLE. — Civilian latrines here chokked up. ii Billet occupied by Motor Machine Gun Section and by R.F.A. Ammn. Column. — in RUE D'AIRE opposite Prison. Recommended that R.F.A be found a new billet as the place is too crowded. Buckets are necessary for latrines. iii Billet occupied by 26th Heavy Battery R.G.A. — No 139 RUE DE LILLE. Condemned as a billet as it is a slaughterer's yard & very filthy.
Feb 9	BETHUNE. Sanitary Section has continued work in town; many loads of refuse being removed. ESSARS Inspected today some billets of the Ox. & Bucks Regt. and

Date	Events

of No 1 Siege Battery R.G.A. Also at LE HAMEL of the 30th Brigade R.F.A (Headquarters, and 15th 48th & 71st Batteries). Arranged with the Adjutant 30th Bge R.F.A. for fatigue parties for work tomorrow and subsequent days.

Cases of MEASLES at VENDIN reported by D.A.D.M.S 1st Division. — about 30 cases altogether, mostly children (no cases of soldiers; village out of bounds for troops) —

Feb 10   Arranged with O.C. No 6 Field Ambulance for a room to be fitted up for sulphur fumigation of blankets.

6 men & 1 NCO of Sanitary Section sent out to ESSARS & LE HAMEL.

BETHUNE   Sanitary work continued.

Feb. 11th.   Work at BETHUNE, ESSARS and LE HAMEL continued.
I again inspected the ORPHANAGE — still a lot of work remains to be done.   Latrine accommodation

Date	Events

(12 buckets) found insufficient, so I ordered use of civilian latrines. This reported to A.D.M.S.

Went to see the Maire of BETHUNE about municipal Sanitary Arrangements, Removal of Horse Manure, and provision of civilian labour.

Promoted L.Corp. Roberts to be acting Corporal, and Privates Clark, Hibblethwaite, Riddell, & Twemlow to be acting L. Corporals.

Feb 12   BETHUNE. Sanitary work continued. Arranged for 10 civilians for tomorrow.
FUMIGATION OF BLANKETS — Capacity of room about 250 – 300 blankets per day. Room ready tomorrow.
LE HAMEL — work continued.

Surveyor from Sanitary Section sent to report on foul ditch at HALTE (9th H.L.I) and on foul drain at GORRE (70th Batt. R.F.A.)

Billet of Divisional Mounted Troops in FAUBOURG D'ARRAS inspected & found satisfactory.

Date	Events
Feb. 13.	Inspected ORPHANAGE with D.A.D.M.S. Very dirty inside. Recommended Coldstream Gds. to transfer to Tobacco Factory. This effected in evening.

Complaint sent in through D.A.D.M.S. of cases where municipal authorities of BETHUNE have not carried out sanitary work properly — all cases cited in report. |
| Feb. 14. | BEUVRY. Went with Capt. Gray to take swabs from meningitis contacts in the Grenadier Gds. Town Commandant BETHUNE is arranging for me to have 20 men permanently for work in BETHUNE. |
| Feb. 15. | BETHUNE. Work continued. Paid 75 francs for civil labour. Maire reported sanitary arrangements complained of on Feb 13 are being done.

Arranged with Capt. Carter 5th Field Ambulance to employ permt. party of his men & 1 or 2 officers. |

Date	Events
Feb 16	BETHUNE. Sanitary work continued. 12 buckets purchased for latrines at Tobacco Factory; wooden seats for the same erected by civilian carpenter. SEVELINGAE and LES CHOQUAUX. 2 parts requiring drainage. Sent out Corp. Roberts to get this work done. BEUVRY 50 men of 5th Field Ambulance & 1 Officer, as well as fatigue party from Irish Gds. worked under direction of Sergt. Tyler in cleaning up this area. Sulphur fumigation room at 6th Field Amb. handed over to Major WINDER.
Feb 17	BETHUNE. & BEUVRY. – work continued as above (Feb 16). Visited billets of Queen's Regt. & of 2nd Grenadier Gds. at BEUVRY. Manure heaps in BETHUNE are being partly removed by civilians to whom I have given permission

Date	Events
Feb 18.	BETHUNE. Received 10 men from A.P.M. for permanent work in the town. Employed them on manure heaps at CHAMPS DE MARS. BEUVRY. - 20 men from No 5 Field Amb. completed the work here. Lieut. WILLIS. has been sent to me for instructional purposes from No 6. Field Ambulance.
Feb 19.	BETHUNE. Arranged with M. LELONG 5g Faubourg M. Pry. to have cesspits at Recreation Room, H.Q. 2nd Divn, the ORPHANAGE, DIVISIONAL MOUNTED TROOPS, and ÉCOLE DE GARÇONS emptied during the next few days. Sent party of men from Sanitary Section to clean up billet of 5th Field Co. R.E. at GORRE.
Feb 20.	BETHUNE. Sanitary work continued. Fitted up an ablution bench at Tobacco Factory.

Date	Events

Feb 21st — Inspected billets of 2nd Signal Co. R.E. and of both batteries R.F.A, both in French barracks in RUE DE LA DELIVRANCE. Straw verminous; recommended discontinuance of use of straw.

BETHUNE. — Sanitary work throughout town continued.

Feb 22nd. Tobacco Factory — now in very good order. More ablution benches fitted up.

Visited this afternoon H.Q. 76th Brigade R.F.A at LE HAMEL; arranged a scheme of drainage to occupy several days' work.

ANNEQUIN. — house where civilian enteric is, has been placed out of bounds; notified A.P.M. and A.D.M.S.

Accumulations of manure at ANNEQUIN were noted.

Feb 23rd. LE HAMEL. Went over area with M.O. and arranged a scheme of drainage. Fatigue party of 30 men from R.F.A.; 10 of my own men & 2 NCO

BETHUNE — rubbish & manure

Date	Events

& removed from Ordnance Stores and from ECOLE DE GARÇONS.

Sample of water from pump in kitchen of HQ 5th Inf. Brigade at LOISNE was taken & forwarded with particulars to Capt. Gray, Bacteriological Laboratory 1st Army.

Feb 24. Visited billets of 35th Heavy R.G.A at LA MOTTE. Billets quite satisfactory but some very dirty ditches require cleaning & draining. Arranged for party of 8 of my orderlies & same number from R.G.A. to start tomorrow on this work under N.C.O.

Similar work continued at LE HAMEL.

BETHUNE. Received notification from A.A. & Q.M.G. that 5 Battalions are coming into BETHUNE. Therefore started to provide latrine & washing accommodation at their billets.

Feb. 25. COLLÈGE DE JEUNES FILLES occupied by Gloucesters & South Wales Borderers of 1st Division last night. Only left in fair condition today. Same thing with 5th Bn King's Regt. at CASERNE

Date	Events

MONTMORENCY.
BETHUNE, LE HAMEL, LA MOTTE, work
continued. Investigated complaint
of civil authorities in BETHUNE about refuse.

Feb 26. The attached statement gives a
summary of the sanitary arrangements
I have provided at the big billets in the
town. A stock of these forms has
been printed and will be used as a
check by the incoming & outgoing
regiments of the sanitary section on
the state of the billets.

BETHUNE, LE HAMEL, LA MOTTE,
work continued.

Feb 27. LE HAMEL, LA MOTTE, work
here almost completed. At some
parts water reduced 18 to 20 inches
in level.
BETHUNE. Sanitary work continued.

Feb. 28 Paid 108 francs to M. LE LONG for
emptying cesspits at Headquarters,
Recreation Room, ECOLE DE GARÇONS
and ORPHANAGE.

12/4/14
March 1915
Summoned but not complied

No 11 Sanitary Officer, 2nd Division

War Diary of
Sanitary Section
2nd Division

March. 1915

Date & Place	Events
BETHUNE March 1st. 1915.	BETHUNE. Billets in the town evacuated by 2nd Inniskilling Fusiliers, 2nd H.L.I, 2nd Worcesters, and 2nd Ox & Bucks L.I. were all left in satisfactory conditions on Feb. 28th. 4th Guards Brigade took over the ORPHANAGE, Tobacco Factory, College de Jeunes Filles, and Caserne Montmorency in a perfectly clean state. LE HAMEL and LAMOTTE. — Drainage Operations continued
Mar 2nd.	Point F 7a on Map, a factory. Case of Diphtheria (1 child) occurred here. Room & clothing have been disinfected by M.O 9th Bat. Child sent to hospital. Billet now occupied by 5th Kings. BETHUNE. Sanitary work continued. Drainage work at LE HAMEL and LAMOTTE completed.

Date	Events
March 3rd.	With A.D.M.S. inspected billets of 5th Kings at Factory by Canal, point F 7a.; and of 1st Herts at VENDIN. 24 handbasins handed over to 1st Irish Guards for washing purposes.
Mar 4	BETHUNE. Sanitary work in town continued.
Mar 5	Inspected billets of 2nd Inniskn. F. at BEUVRY. Latrine accommodation of C & D Companies very restricted. Buckets required. Various heaps of refuse & manure to be removed. B & C companies were overcrowded; recommended that more room be found them as on March 7 the refugees in the village have to move out. Straw for those floors required. BETHUNE. 1st Herts Regt completed the moving of their battalion to VENDIN from College de Jeunes Filles.

Date, Place	Events.
Mar 6th BETHUNE.	BEUVRY. The sanitary work mentioned in yesterday's report was carried out today by party of men from BETHUNE with 1 waggon.

BETHUNE. Store of implements – shovels, spades, brushes, wheelbarrows, forks etc., – has been got together at my office so that Units can borrow from it. This notified in Routine orders.
One case of Cerebro Spinal Meningitis at No 6 Field Ambulance dealt with. Room fumigated & cleaned out with Cresol.
List of Water Carts in 2nd Division sent in to A.D.M.S. |
Mar 7.	Sanitary work in BETHUNE continued.
Mar 8.	With A.D.M.S. visited billets of Inniskilling Fusiliers at BEUVRY to point out cases of overcrowding. Stricter supervision of drinking water found to be necessary.
Mar 9th	Sent in to Town Commandant and

Date	Events
	to D.A.Q.M.G 2nd Divn a complete list of those places in BETHUNE found by my men where more troops could be accommodated. Total accommodation found was approx. for 800 men.

Visited ORPHANAGE, & CASERNE MONTMORENCY and found sanitary work proceeding satisfactorily. |
| Mar 10. | During night all big billets in BETHUNE were evacuated by 4th Brigade in anticipation of this morning's attack by us. All men of Sanitary Section, 11 prisoners & 19 men of fatigue party were therefore engaged in cleaning up billets. 5 civilian carts employed and 9 teams of horses and drivers from 2nd Divisional Train. |
| Mar 11 | ANNEQUIN. Visited Brig. Gen. Chichester, 5th Brigade in regard to sanitation of his area. With M.O. of 9th H.L.I. inspected billets at ANNEQUIN. |

Events.

12th BETHUNE. — Sanitary work continued.

Large demands made by 6th Inf. Brigade on my store of implements.
Inspected billets of 1st Berks. at CASERNE MONTMORENCY with their M.O.

Mar. 13. Visited trenches at CUINCHY with M.O. 2nd H.L.I (Armstrong). to see latrines & sanitary state generally. Sent in report on this to A.D.M.S. This put in Routine Orders for next day.
Motor lorry lent to O.C. 1st Kings at 6.30 p.m. for conveyance of burial party to PONT FIXE.

Mar 14 Diphtheria case at BEUVRY investigated. — Pte MULLAN 2nd Inneskilling Fusiliers; Section isolated; cannot disinfect the Gymnasium in which he was.
BETHUNE — Sanitary work continued.

Mar 15. BEUVRY. Waggon & N.C.O sent out to M.O. 2nd Innisk. F. for

Date	Events
	removing refuse from billets & streets.
	BETHUNE – Sanitary work as usual.
Mar 16.	BEUVRY. – work as yesterday.
	BETHUNE. – work as usual.
	Visited LE QUESNOY to investigate & plan a scheme of drainage of some dirty ditches there. Arranged with C.O. 2nd Coldstream Gds. for a fatigue party tomorrow.
Mar 17	LE QUESNOY. – drainage work.
	Visited LE PREOL to see if bucket latrines are necessary (a request for same was received from M.O. 2nd Grenadier Guards).
	BEUVRY. – work as yesterday.
	BETHUNE – Sanitary work continued
Mar 18.	With A.D.M.S. visited billets of 2nd D.A.C. and Supply Columns at LABEUVRIÈRE. All billets satisfactory.
	LE QUESNOY. Drainage operations continued.
	Specimen trench latrines were

Date	Events
	cut today by working party on high ground in RUE DES SABLIÈRES. and were put open to investigation of Company Officers & M.Os. of 6th Inf. Brigade now in BETHUNE.
Mar 19	LABEUVRIÈRE — ditches cleaned out under direction of Sanitary N.CO.
	LE QUESNOY — work continued.
	BETHUNE — Sanitary work continued ECOLE MICHELET. Report by M.O. South Staffords re gas pipes, water taps & drains. All attended to today.
Mar 20	BETHUNE. Sanitary work continued Refuse removed from all big billets.
	W.C. at General Horne's billet attended to.
	Leak of gas at Divisional Headquarters put right.
	Handed over work to Capt. Renshaw R.A.M.C. when I went on leave.

To
The A.D.M.S.
   2nd Division

Sanitary Report

The following billets were evacuated to-day.
1. The Tobacco Factory
2. Ecole de Jeunes Filles
3. Ecole Michelet

All the above billets were thoroughly cleaned with the aid of fatigue parties from the regiments in occupation.

One load of Refuse was removed from 2nd Sig. Coy. Rue de L'armée.

One load of refuse removed from N°. Quarters of 2nd Sig. Coy.

Montmorency Barracks were evacuated to-day. The Barracks were thoroughly cleaned and all rubbish burnt.
Four loads of Manure & two loads of refuse were removed from these Barracks.

The work of cleaning ditches at LE QUESNOY has been completed.

The refuse removed from ditches at
LE QUESNOY is to be removed by a
fatigue party of the Coldstream Guards.

J W Tunshaw
Capt RAMC
for Sant. Officer...
2nd Division

21 3/15

To
A.D.M.S
  2nd Division

Sanitary Report

Removed one load manure and two loads refuse from Montmorency Barracks. All other refuse burnt.

The Orphanage & the École de Jeunes Filles were vacated this afternoon. Most of the refuse was removed, and both billets were left clean.

The billet occupied by Left Section 56th Battery is being cleaned with the aid of a fatigue party from the battery. There is a large collection of manure in the yard of this billet which will take some days to remove.

One load of manure removed from M.M.P. Stables

All horses from 35th Coy ASC were taken away today at 11 a.m. which prevented any further removal of manure being carried out.

22/3/15

J A Renshaw
for Capt Rawl
for Sant. Officer 2nd Div

To ADMS
2nd Division

There are about 20 water closets in the
École de Jeunes Filles several of which
are damaged & not in use.
Seven of these are not in use as the flush
is out of order.
Three have the pans broken
In one case the pipe leaks.
From what I can ascertain all these
water-closets were out of order when
the 2nd Division took over.
They have all been nailed up except
for three which have been left for
officers use only.
Except for the three mentioned for
officers use, these water closets have
always been nailed up since the 2nd
Division took over, but in many
instances the doors have been forced
& an attempt made to use them.
A more careful observation will be
made for the future to see that doors
are not forced open & use made of these
water closets.

23/3/15

Jas Renshaw
Capt RAMC
pro Sant Off 2nd Div

To
The ADMS
2nd Division

One load of manure removed from M.M.P stables & taken to Boul'd Thiers —

One load of rubbish removed from refilling point —

All rubbish removed from École de jeune filles —

Billet occupied by officer of D.W Troops who had measles, has been disinfected.

Seven loads of manure removed from H.Quarter Stables —

Saw A.P.M with reference to a case of Enteric fever that has occurred just beyond ANNEQUIN in a billet shown on Map Square B 23 B.

The case is a French child, and the A.P.M has ordered the Mayor to have the case sent to a civil Hosp in the interest of the Troops.

Ten loads of manure removed from billet occupied by left section 56th Battery R.F.A shown on Map Square A 20 C.

23/3/15

J.A Renshaw
Capt R.A.M.C
for Sant officer 2nd Div

To
The A.D.M.S.
2nd Division

The Orphanage was vacated today by the
Cameron Highlanders — Billets clean & refuse
has been removed.
All refuse removed from Tobacco Factory
& Ecole Michelet.

Eighteen loads of manure were removed
from billet occupied by 56" Battery R.F.A.
Map square A 20 C.

Two loads of rubbish removed from
the Refilling Point.

One load of rubbish & two of manure
removed from Montmorency Barracks

One load of rubbish removed from
Ecole Repl Bert.
One load manure removed from Hd quart.
Signalling Coy & two loads from Champs
de Mars

24 3/15

Jas Renshaw
Capt Rame
for Sant Officer
2nd Div

To ADMS
2nd Division — Sanitary Report

Removed six cartloads of manure from billet occupied by left section 56th Battery R.F.A. - Map square A 20 C 5.8
Removed 16 cartloads from billet shown on map square A 20 C 5.5 also occupied by 56th Battery R.F.A.

Removed a load of rubbish from No 15 Boulevard Thier
Three loads rubbish removed from Tobacco Factory and Orphenage
Two loads rubbish removed from École de jeune Filles.
The part of the École de jeune Filles at present unoccupied is being scrubbed out with Cresol solution
Assistance is being given by prisoner obtained from the Town Commandant
All water closets except three have been fastened up.

Two loads of rubbish removed from refilling point.

six cartloads of manure removed from Champ de Mars.

JA Renshaw
Capt REME
for Equerry Officer
2nd Division

To
ADMS
2nd Division   Sanitary Report

Removed 16 cart loads manure from billet of
56th Battery R.F.A. - Map Square A 20 C 5·5.

Two loads of rubbish removed from Tobacco
Factory & Ecole Michelet -
Trench closets at the Orphanage have been
fastened up.
One load of ashes carted from Gasworks
to Orphanage for the purpose of laying
on the Ground round wash basins -

30 yds of Canvas screen have been placed
round latrine in Ecole de jeune Fille -
Old urine pits have been filled in and
new ones dug.
Two loads of rubbish removed from
Ecole de jeune filles -

Essars
Ditches near billets occupied by A.S.C.
have been cleaned out with the aid of
a small fatigue party - Map Square
X 25 a 8·2. - All refuse has been
burned in a field near by.

One load of rubbish removed from the
Refilling point -
One load of manure removed from Physics
and Chemistry College -

One load of rubbish & one of manure
removed from Montmorency Barracks

Seven loads of manure were removed
from the Champ de Mars.

J A Tench ay?
Capt. R a u l s
for San'y Officer
2nd Division

26 3/15

To
The ADMS   <u>Sanitary Report</u>
   2nd Division

Two loads of rubbish removed from Orphanage, Ecole Michelet & Tobacco Factory.
One load of cinders carted from Gas works to Orphanage.
The Ecole Michelet was vacated to day with the exception of the Guardroom. The billet is clean & ready for occupation.
A start has been made at emptying the cesspools at the Orphanage. This should be finished tomorrow.

Two loads of refuse removed from the Refilling point.

One load of rubbish & one of manure removed from Mont Morency Barracks.

Seven loads of manure removed from Champ de Mars.
Eighteen loads of manure removed from billets of 56th Battery R.F.A. Main square. A 20 C.C.S.
Two loads of rubbish removed from Ecole de jeune fille.

The gas supply has been cut off from the right wing of the École de Jeune Fille pending repairs to fittings.

The load of rubbish removed from 15 Boulevard Thiers & some chloride of lime sprinkled on ground.

The work of clearing ditches on the Sisar Béthune Road has been completed. All refuse &c removed has been buried.

27 3/11

pd Truchaw
Cap. Raue
for Sanity Officer
2nd Division

To
The ADMS   Sanitary Report
    2nd Division

Four loads of rubbish removed from Tobacco Factory, Ecole Michelet & Orphanage.

One load of rubbish removed from Ecole de Jeune Filles — All rubbish such as paper & straw etc was burnt in incinerator.

Four loads of manure removed from the Champs de Mars.

Two loads of rubbish removed from refilling point.

Twelve loads manure removed from billets of 56th Battery R.F.A. A 26 A 5.9

Incinerator in grounds of Physics & Chemistry College repaired.

Billets of Ad. Quarter Staff & East Anglian Coy R.E. in Pontifrai Rd. Map square A 20 B 2.4 was cleaned — all rubbish burnt. Other billets occupied by this unit

being cleaned by a fatigue party
furnished by the unit, under the super-
-vision of an NCO of the Sanitary Section

28 3/11 -

J H Renshaw
Capt. RAMC
for Sanit. Officer
2nd Divn

Date.	Events.

Mar 29. Returned from leave to duty in morning.
BETHUNE. Inspected billets in town.
Floors at ECOLE JEUNES FILLES scrubbed with cresol solution.
BEUVRY. Moat farm. The moat has been cleared of floating refuse.
CAMBRIN. — work continued; carting manure from billet of 56th Battery R.F.A.

Mar 30 CAMBRIN. — work continued.
EAST ANGLIAN Field Co. R.E at PONT FIXE Road. Have arranged with M.O. Divnl Engineers to send out a party daily here till work of cleaning up these very dirty billets is finished.
BEUVRY — I visited Chateau Farm re the moat.
BETHUNE Inspected ORPHANAGE with M.O. 6th London Rifles.

Date	Events

Mar 31st — In morning with A.D.M.S. visited ESSARS and LE HAMEL to arrange scheme for further drainage of dirty water in ditches.

CAMBRIN. 4 men & 1 N.C.O employed today (EAST ANGLIAN Billet)

BETHUNE.
4 more carts hired for work of removing refuse and for dealing with accumulations of refuse at Refilling Point. Total Number of Carts & Waggons now employed is 9.
More men still required for sanitary work in town. Sent in request for 10 more men to A.D.M.S.

James Clayton
Lieut. R.A.M.C.
O.C. Sanitary Section
2nd Divn.

BETHUNE.
31.3.15.

15/4 1913

nil 5294
April 14/15

121/5294

Summoned but not copied

No 11. Sanitary Officer, 2nd Division

War Diary

of

Sanitary Officer

2nd Division

To A.D.M.S. 2nd Div.

Report of Sanitary Officer.   April 1st. 1915.

BETHUNE. Sanitary work and removal of refuse from all parts of town continued.

At the ORPHANAGE, twelve more bucket latrines with seats have been supplied today.

At ECOLE MICHELET. an ablution bench is in course of erection.

I have visited M. SARRUT, Directeur des Travaux Municipaux re having drains in town flushed more frequently. He states that he is allowed only a certain quantity of water per week for this purpose, and flushing takes place on 3 days in the week. Householders are responsible for the cleanliness of the part of the gutter immediately in front of their houses. I enquired about the use of a cart for brushing the streets and one for watering the streets in dry weather. He can probably let me have these in a few days.

EAST ANGLIAN Field Co. R.E. Billets on Pont Fixe Road. I sent out a party of 2 N.C.Os + 16 men to work here today. Work not yet completed.

ANNEZIN. 1 N.CO. sent out to see to cleaning of drain reported to me by D.A.D.M.S.

CHATEAU FARM, BEUVRY. 1 N.CO. sent out to see to cleaning of dirty ditch alongside road here.

James Clayton
Lieut. R.A.M.C.

A.D.M.S. 2nd Div.
Report of Sanitary Officer. April 2nd

BETHUNE., ANNEZIN., BEUVRY, PONT
FIXE — work same as yesterday

James Clayton
Lieut. RAMC

To A.D.M.S. 2nd Div.

Report of Sanitary Officer.   April 3rd, 1915.

CAMBRIN.   14 men under 1 N.C.O. have worked at billets of East Anglian Field Co. R.E., burying refuse, cleaning out cesspools & disinfecting a house.

BETHUNE.
With A.D.M.S. 2nd Div. I inspected billets at ORPHANAGE and Tobacco Factory. Suggestion received that bucket latrines & seats be covered in to protect men from wet. This will be done.

Refilling Point. 32 cart loads of refuse have been removed from here today. The QUAI — used as part of Refilling Point — was not brushed up by A.S.C. after their work was done.

James Clayton
Lieut. R.A.M.C.

To A.D.M.S. 2nd Division.
Report of Sanitary Officer. April 4th 1915.

CAMBRIN. 10 men + 1 N.C.O. employed on billets of East Anglian Field Co. R.E. and on 1 house in which are 1. Staffords.

BETHUNE.
Refilling Point. 8 men, + 1 N.C.O. and 4 carts employed carting refuse away. The side roads leading to the QUAI and part of the QUAI itself has not been swept up today by A.S.C. men.

ECOLE JEUNES FILLES. — 5 loads of ashes carted from ANNEZIN to the above billet for use in making a clean pathway at back.

Refuse removed from all billets in town.

James Clayton
Lieut. R.A.M.C.

To A.D.M.S. 2nd Division

Report of Sanitary Officer.   April 5th 1915.

BETHUNE.

Refuse removed from all big billets in BETHUNE and from Refilling Point and manure from Champ de Mars etc.

Several loads of ashes have been carted from ANNEZIN to the ECOLE JEUNES FILLES to provide clean paths there.

I have obtained two horses and drivers from No.4 Field Ambulance, to work the machine brush and watering cart and have personally seen that these things are in working order.

The special work in the town on which some of my men are at present engaged consists of

The erection of Ablution benches, taps etc at ECOLE JEUNES FILLES,

Tobacco Factory and ECOLE MICHELET.

The erection of covers to all the latrines (total of 96 buckets) at ORPHANAGE, TOBACCO FACTORY, ECOLE JEUNES FILLES, and CASERNE MONTMORENCY. This will take about a week to complete.

I took a party of 12 Officers of the 1st Herts including their C.O., to see the TRENCH LATRINE specimens.

Working parties have been engaged today as follows:—

CAMBRIN — 9 men + 1 N.C.O.

BEUVRY — 26th Heavy R.G.A Waggon lines, 4 men and 1 N.C.O.

James Clayton
Lieut. R.A.M.C.

To A.D.M.S. 2nd Divn.

Report of Sanitary Officer.   April 6th 1915.

BETHUNE.   All arrangements have been made for representatives of the Sanitary Section to be in attendance at the billets which will be vacated tomorrow at 7.30 to 8.30 a.m. by the 6th, 7th and 8th London Battalions, in order to see that they are left in a clean state.

The 1st Herts Battalion vacated the ECOLE JEUNES FILLES today and left it clean.

In connection with the covering in of all bucket latrines, a large amount of wood has been obtained through the Requisitioning Officer. The work will probably take a week to complete and will be carried out by men of the Sanitary Section.

The Rotary Machine Brush has been at work at the yards of the ORPHANAGE, TOBACCO FACTORY and ECOLE JEUNES FILLES, and it works quite satisfactorily.

Ashes continue to be carted from ANNEZIN to the ECOLE JEUNES FILLES.

CAMBRIN. — Work here continued with 9 men and 1 N.C.O. Large amounts of refuse have been collected together from billets in Harley Street and have been dumped in a field where the refuse will be treated with chloride of lime and then covered with earth.

BEUVRY. I visited the billets of 26th Heavy R.G.A. There are some very bad cesspools here and drains which are very foul. About 50 yards of tile drains will be necessary to carry out the work properly, and work will be carried on for several days. 6 men & 1 N.CO employed here today. Two cases of suspected Diphtheria were sent in from here some time ago.

CHAMPS DE MARS. Specimen

Latrines filled in. Refuse collected and carted away. The refuse has been thrown here by civilian occupants of 2 houses. They are being dealt with. The small incinerator at this place is one built temporarily each day by men of Field Ambulance for burning old dressings.

James Clayton
Lieut. RAMC

A.D.M.S. 2nd Div.

Report of Sanitary Officer.   April 7th 1915.

BETHUNE.   Sanitary work at all big
   billets continued.
6th, 7th + 8th London Battalions
left billets today ;   billet of 18th
London left dirty.   Reported to
Town Commandant.
Other work in the town ; - Sawing
+ carrying lumber for latrines.

~~CUCHY~~.   With A.D.M.S. visited
   LAMOTTE, ESSARS, and
2nd D.A.C. at FOUQUEREUIL.

CAMBRN   1 N.C.O + 9 men.

26th Heavy R.G.A.   1 N.C.O + 4 men

       Francis Clayton
       Lieut. RAMC

To A.D.M.S. 2nd Divn
Report of Sanitary Officer. April 8th/15.

BETHUNE.
Refuse removed from all big billets.
Rotary Machine Brush employed at billets and in the town.
Refilling Point has now been cleared of all old accumulation of refuse.
2 carts and 10 men obtained today from 15th London Battalion for cartage of ashes from ANNEZIN to ECOLE JEUNES FILLES.

CAMBRIN. 9 men and 1 N.CO.
Still employed clearing refuse from billets. Work to be completed tomorrow.

BEUVRY. 4 men & 1 N.CO.
Employed at billets of 20th Heavy R.G.A. building an incinerator, filling up old

cesspits, and draining
a very dirty yard.

James Clayton
Lieut. RAMC

To A.D.M.S. 2nd Division
Report of Sanitary Officer.   April 9th.

ESSARS and LA MOTTE.   10 men and
2 N.C.O.s employed here today on the work of draining ditches etc planned out a few days ago. Tomorrow at least 18 men will be employed. I started these at work myself at 9.30 am.
The C.R.E. has promised to let me have 2 force pumps tomorrow afternoon about 4 or 5 pm.

CAMBRIN.   1 N.C.O and 5 men at work on Harley Street today. One day's work in covering up refuse still remains.

BETHUNE.   The following work was continued today.
Removed refuse from all big

billets and Refilling Point and of manure from Champ de Mars and from 6th Field Ambulance Stables.
Cartage of red shale and bricks for incinerators from ANNEZIN.
Cartage of wood purchased to saw mill for sawing into posts and planks for covering all latrines.

36 more latrine seats have been set up at ECOLE DE JEUNES FILLES.

BEUVRY. 1 N.CO and 4 men still engaged on billet of 26th Heavy R.G.A.

James Clayton
Lieut. R.Ome.

To A.D.M.S. 2nd Division.

Report of Sanitary Officer April 10th.

BETHUNE.

All refuse removed from big billets in the town.

(1) Manure has been removed continuously by my men from Champs de Mars but as there are approximately 400 horses here, manure tends to accumulate. I have therefore written to O.C. of 56th and 47th Batteries R.F.A., 44th Brigade Amm: Column and 2nd Signal Co, R.E., whose horses are here to see if they can arrange to cart away their own manure.

CIVILIAN LABOUR.

(2) The Maire of BETHUNE says he can provide about 50 civilians in two or three days for work at 3 francs a day, working from 8am to 12 am and 1.30 pm to 4.30 pm.

48

ESSARS. 16 men and 1 N.C.O. employed here today. Good progress with the drainage has been made, the drains having been opened up and the water flowing in them is now clean fresh water.

As regards the open cesspit, enquiries have been made and it was found that there is a continuous flow into and out of this dirty cesspit. If this were filled in with road scrapings, the water would flow out and spread on to the ground.

(3) The billet at ESSARS previously put out of bounds on account of infectious disease is now occupied by men of the Royal Inniskilling Fusiliers. The billet itself is not nearly so dirty as formerly as the

50

...owner is at present engaged in carting out the manure from the central yard.

LA MOTTE. 4 men & 1 N.C.O. employed. One hilet has been completed.

CAMBRIN. 5 men & 1 N.C.O. completed work of clearing refuse from Harley Street. The refuse has been put into a heap in a field, & covered with chloride of lime and earth.

In BETHUNE the work of covering all latrines proceeds.

James Clayton
Lieut. R.A.M.C.

To A.D.M.S. 2nd Division.

Report of Sanitary Officer. April 11th 1915.

BETHUNE.
Refuse removed from all big billets. Manure removed from Champ de Mars and from stables of H.Q. Officers.

LATRINE COVERN. Work is proceeding satisfactorily at the Tobacco Factory. At the ORPHANAGE, the O.C. London Irish has promised me the use of his Pioneers for helping to carry out the work tomorrow.

BEUVRY. Work at billet of 26th Heavy R.G.A. is now completed.
ESSARS. 18 men and 2 N.COs employed on drainage work today.
LA MOTTE. 4 men & 1 N.CO. employed on the second farm today.
Two force pumps have been

lent me for this drainage work by the 5th Field Co. R.E. at GORRE.

James Clayton
Lieut. R.A.M.C.

To A.D.M.S. 2nd Divn.
Report of Sanitary Officer - April 12th/15.

BETHUNE. Refuse removed from all big billets and from
H.Q. Royal Artillery.
No 15 Boulevard Thiers (previously occupied by Officers of Post Office Rifles)
Nos. 77 and 51 Rue Victor Hugo — previously used as Brigade H.Q. and now H.Q. of 5th London Brigade.

I have stopped removing manure from Champ de Mars as Major Ready has now ordered the Units in occupation to remove their manure to places specified by me; instead, I have commenced carting the large heap of manure in Boulevard Thiers of which the Maire complained.

LATRINE COVERS. Those at Tobacco Factory are completed. Work commenced today on those at ORPHANAGE and at CASERNE MONTMORENCY.

I have purchased today some forks (for handling manure) in Lillers but no buckets or suitable broom heads were obtainable. The D.A.D.O.S. has asked for a large supply of latrine buckets and bass broom heads to be sent up from the Base.

At ESSARS and LA MOTTE, 2 N.C.Os and 22 men have been employed.

James Clayton
Lieut. R.E.

A.D.M.S. 2nd Divs.
Report of Sanitary Officer. April 13th 1915

BETHUNE.

Refuse removed from all by billets, and from 77 and 51 Rue Victor Hugo and H.Q. Divisional R.A.

I have notified the O.S.C. of 17th London Regt. and of 5th London Brigade that they must remove the manure of their Units in the town to the field by French Flying Ground.

18 cart loads of manure removed from Boulevard Thiers.

ESSARS and LA MOTTE.

2 N.C.Os and 22 men engaged on work here today.

I have visited LE HAMEL, have gone over some of the work to be done there with the O.C. 36th Brigade R.F.A and have arranged to send out men from ESSARS as soon as they can be spared.

James Clayton
Lieut. R.A.M.C.

To A.D.M.S. 2nd Division.

Report of Sanitary Officer. April 14th

Went with D.A.D.O.S. to Amiens to purchase 2 large pumps & sprays for spraying manure heaps to keep down flies.

Work carried on by Sanitary Section as yesterday.

J Clayton
Lieut. RAMC.

A.D.M.S. 2nd Div.
Report of Sanitary Officer. April 30th 1915

BETHUNE. Visited Chicory Factory & Sausage Factory both in the Rue de LILLE in the morning. The latter place is in a disgusting condition and is a menace to the health of troops & civilians. I have asked the Town Commandant to place this place out of bounds for troops & also to approach the French authorities with a view to exercising some municipal control over the place.

Sanitary work in the town continued as usual, about 70 men being employed. All new billets of 6th Brigade in the town have been inspected, and where necessary arrangements made for removal of refuse & manure.

BEUVRY, CAMBRIN & LE HAMEL work as yesterday.

J. Clayton
Lieut R.A.M.C.

A.D.M.S. 2nd Divn.

Report of Sanitary Officer. April 15th.

BETHUNE. Work of removing refuse and manure in the town carried on as usual.

ÉCOLE DE JEUNES FILLES.

I have to report that the left hand part of the billet occupied by the 19th London Battalion was this morning in a very unsatisfactory state. Neither the Adjutant, Orderly Officer, nor the M.O. could be found on application at the Orderly Room, so that the state of the billet could be pointed out to them. The yard occupied by the transport of the battalion contained heaps of mud and refuse; refuse in the basement pointed out yesterday had not been removed, and the room

in which the case of measles
occurred had not been scrubbed
out with creosol after 2 days.
I suggest that these matters be
brought to the notice of the O.C.
Battalion.

ESSARS and LA MOTTE

2 N.C.Os and 22 men worked
here today.

2 pumps and sprays were
purchased yesterday for spraying
manure heaps. They work
quite satisfactorily.

James Clayton
Lieut. R.A.M.

A.D.M.S. 2nd Div.

Report of Sanitary Officer.   April 16. 1915.

BETHUNE.
Refuse removed from all big billets in the town. Manure removed from Boulevard Thiers and Police Stables. Refuse from Refilling Point removed. Rotary Brush and Watering Cart employed at some of yards of billets and at Refilling Point.

LATRINE COVERS at Tobacco Factory, CASERNE MONTMORENCY and ORPHANAGE are now finished. The ground at ECOLE DE JEUNES FILLES is being prepared for latrines in a new position.

ECOLE JEUNES FILLES. I again visited this billet and pointed out accumulations of refuse & dirt to the M.O. 19th London Regt. and to the Adjutant 15th London Regt. Both are leaving tomorrow.

The W.C. notified to me has been cleaned out and screwed up, as also one in the building itself. It is proposed to put down a concrete and brick flooring for the space now occupied by the washing benches in the right hand half of the building.

BASSARS and LA MOTTE.

2 NCOs & 22 men employed at these places. I visited both and saw that very satisfactory work is being done.

GORRE. The Rotary Brush here belongs to M. CLEMENT, Chef Cantonnier SAILLY LA BOURSE, from whom permission to use it must be obtained.

J. Clayton
Lieut R.E.

To A.D.M.S. 2nd Divn.

Report of Sanitary Officer. April 17th 1915.

BETHUNE. Refuse removed from all big billets and Refilling Point.

ECOLE JEUNES FILLES. Ground is being prepared for latrines in a new position previous to covering over the latrines. The floor of the washing place is being set with bricks in concrete.

ECOLE MICHELET. Washing room at this billet has been opened.

Orders have been issued that all burnable refuse and tins must first be passed through the incinerator before being carted away.

Boulevard Thiers. Manure carted away from here. Orders were given to Sergt. Major of 3rd F.A. that manure from his stables must now be carted away to the field near the French flying ground.

BEUVRY. I visited billet of 19th London Battery. The M.O. was not present, but Lieut. in charge promised to have manure removed and billet left clean before vacating tonight.

Billet of Lieut. Hewett 1st Royal Berks was put out of bounds and Adjt. of 1st Kings notified of the same.

James Clayton
Lieut. RAMC

To A.D.M.S. 2nd Div.

Report of Sanitary Officer. April 18th 1915.

BETHUNE. Sanitary work, removal of refuse and manure continued as usual.

ESSARS. 1 N.C.O. & 5 men continued work here on large open cesspit, and have emptied it completely and put bricks in the bottom. It will probably be completed tomorrow.

~~ESSARS~~ LE HAMEL. 1 N.C.O. and 20 men were sent out here yesterday & are billetted with 36th Brigade R.F.A. They are working on the ditches and large manure heaps in 4 farms and are employing 2 large pumps, and 4 carts with horses. I visited this place today to see that work was proceeding satisfactorily. I also went to ESSARS, and to

5th London Amm. Column at ECLUSE D'ENARS to investigate case of scarlet fever reported yesterday. This place was very dirty so spoke to O.C. about it and ordered rooms to be all cleaned & refuse burnt; blankets to be sent to No.6. F.A. for disinfection at once. Am sending a man tomorrow to disinfect the rooms.

CHATEAU GORRE. Visited this and arranged with Adjutant to have whole place thoroughly cleaned up, refuse collected & burnt, tins buried, and all manure outside and in central yard carted away to fields.

CHAMBOID BARRACKS, BETHUNE.

Disinfected room which had case of measles reported from 2nd Signal Co. R.E.

Also disinfected room at ORPHANAGE in which case of measles occurred.

J. Clayton
Lieut. RAMC.

To A.D.M.S. 2nd Div.
Report of Sanitary Officer.   April 19th 1915.

BETHUNE.   Sanitary work continued.

All manure has now been removed from Boulevard Thiers.
Disinfections of rooms (measles cases) have been carried out at the ORPHANAGE, ECOLE DE JEUNES FILLES, and 5th London Ammn. Column at ECLUSE D'ESSARS.

ESSARS.   1 N.C.O. and 5 men; finished work on cesspit.

LE HAMEL.   2 N.C.Os and 20 men working here today.

Visited BEUVRY this afternoon in response to request from O.C. 2nd Heavy R.G.A. to see manure heaps & cesspits and to give advice. I also inspected the billets occupied by the Transport of

5th Kings Liverpools. Some of these were very dirty, and the Officer in charge knew nothing of the orders concerning removal of manure. These orders were shown him and he arranged for a start to be made in cleaning up the billets and removing manure. Also visited the Maire of BEUVRY and tried to get him to prevent civilians from throwing refuse into the streets and gutters.

James Clayton
Lieut. R.Army

A.D.M.S. 2nd Div.
Report of Sanitary Officer   April 20. 1915.

BETHUNE.   All billets of Battalions of
2nd London Division T.F. were evacuated
yesterday and left in a clean condition.
Removal of refuse & manure from
all big billets carried out.

LE HAMEL.   2 N.C.Os + 20 men employed
here.

BEUVRY.   1 N.C.O and 10 men employed
carting away refuse from the
central square and in cleansing
out ditches noticed yesterday.

J Clayton
Lieut. R.A.M.C.

A.D.M.S. 2nd Div.
Report of Sanitary Officer.   April 21st /1915.

BETHUNE.

Removal of refuse and sanitary work in town continued.
For the more effective carrying out of the work of removal of refuse it is proposed to substitute single horse carts for those 2 or 3 large waggons now in use. One single horse cart is almost as effective as one 4-horse waggon. The difficulty arises that neither the Field Ambulances nor the Divisional Train have any more single horse harness. Can a recommendation for purchase of the same be made?

Cesspits at several places in the town now urgently require emptying, but the civilian apparatus previously employed to do this work cannot be depended upon as it is stated to have broken down. The supply of a similar apparatus directly under my control is absolutely necessary.

Supply of Materials for treating manure heaps.

I have arranged with the Supply Officer 2nd Div. for a weekly supply of 56 gallons Paraffin; also for expediting the supply of Borax and Formalin recently ordered.

CIVILIAN LABOUR. Authority now given me by Major Ready for employment of 50 civilians. The Maire of BETHUNE is collecting these together for me. I hope to have them in 2 days' time.

BEUVRY. 1 N.C.O + 10 men employed as yesterday.

LE HAMEL. 2 N.C.O + 20 men employed as yesterday.

J. Clayton
Lieut. R.A.M.C

To A.D.M.S. 2nd Division.

Report of Sanitary Officer. April 22nd 1915.

BETHUNE. Refuse removed from all big billets and from Refilling Point, Divisional Mounted Troops, Military Police billet, 2nd Signal Co. billet, and from Boot Repairing Billet and yard of Hotel de France.

Manure removed from Champ de Mars, Military Police Stables and H.Q. Stables in Boulevard Thiers, and Place de Lille. Sanitary work in the town also continued. Total number of men employed in the town approx. 60 and of carts or waggons 7.

Divisional Mounted Troops. A very large heap of manure exists here and as this will take a long time to cart away, it will be treated with borax or paraffin.

Cesspits urgently require emptying at several billets in the town. To get this work done more speedily, I visited first M. LELONG whose apparatus we employ & then the Maire whose officials promised help.

CASE OF MEASLES 35th Heavy R.G.A I located at LA MOTTE. Disinfection will be carried out tomorrow.

BEUVRY. 1 N.C.O & 70 men employed as yesterday finished this particular work.

LE HAMEL 1 N.C.O and 12 men employed as yesterday.

James Clayton
Lieut. R.A.M.C.

A.D.M.S. 2nd Div.

Report of Sanitary Officer.   April, 23rd. 1915.

BETHUNE. Sanitary work in the town continued as usual, refuse and manure being removed from billets and all parts of the town.

23 civilians were employed today cleaning up at the chief refuse tip; in cleaning out dirty ditches, and in making a new channel for the waste water from the ablution bench at ORPHANAGE.

Large heap of manure at Divisional Mounted Troops billet has been sprayed with 5% Borax Solution.

Cess pits have been emptied at the ORPHANAGE and TOBACCO FACTORY; several others remain to be done.

The work of providing new latrine and washing accommodation at ECOLE DE JEUNES FILLES is proceeding satisfactorily.

BEUVRY. 2 N.C.Os and 14 men with carts have been employed on new work of carting manure from farmyards, pumping out cesspits etc. This work here will take several days.

LE HAMEL. 1 N.C.O. and 12 men employed as yesterday.

James Clayton
Lieut. R.A.M.C.

A.D.M.S. 2nd Div.
Report of Sanitary Officer. April 24th 1915

BETHUNE Sanitary work in town; removal of refuse and manure continued. Approximately 60 men being employed.

Several big billets in BETHUNE were vacated by Units today, those of the 7th London Battalion T.F. at ECOLE MICHELET being left in a very dirty state. A strongly worded recommendation was forwarded

to Div. H.Q. through Town Commandant that a fatigue party from this Battalion be brought back to clean up.

Cesspits at ECOLE MICHELET have been emptied today; 4 others remain to be done.

If more troops come into the town it will be absolutely necessary to procure more carts, horses & drivers for the removal of refuse and manure.

23 civilians were also employed in the town today on similar work to yesterday's.

BEUVRY.   2 N.COs & 14 men employed as yesterday.

LE HAMEL.   1 N.C.O. and 12 men employed as yesterday.

James Clayton
Lieut. R.A.M.C.

A.D.M.S. 2nd Div.

Report of Sanitary Officer. April 25th 1915.

BETHUNE. Sanitary work in town continued. Refuse and manure removed from all big billets. All manure has now been removed from Champ de Mars. Arrangements have further been made for the regular removal by the Sanitary Section of manure from those stables where no transport exists i.e. those under the command of the Camp Commandant.

Civilian labour. No civilians were employed today; 50 will be employed tomorrow.

BEUVRY. Manure removed from billets of 17th Battery R.F.A. 2 NCOs and 14 men being employed.

LE HAMEL. 1 N.CO. and 12 men still employed by 36th Brigade R.F.A.

J. Clayton
Lieut R.A.M.C.

A.D.M.S. 2nd Div.

Report of Sanitary Officer. April 24th 1915

BETHUNE. Work carried out as usual in the town, approximately 60 men being employed.

Inspections were carried out by N.Cos of Sanitary Section of the new billetting areas occupied by the Worcesters by the Canal and by the Oxf & Bucks (Faubourg St. Pry) and of Rue Faubourg D'Arras.

I have shown the Sanitary Officer 2nd London Division all the sanitary arrangements we have in the town.

Disinfections of billets have been carried out at LE PREOL (15th London Regt), VENDIN (2nd Div. Train) and at billet of D.M. Troops the Clock Factory occupied by the Cyclists.

BEUVRY. 2 N.Cos & 14 men

employed at billets of 17th Battery R.F.A. & at Transport of 5th Kings removing manure, pumping out cesspits etc.

LE HAMEL   1 N.C.O. and 12 men still employed.

CIVILIANS.   50 civilians worked today at BEUVRY, the Orphanage and elsewhere removing manure, cleaning out ditches etc.

James Clayton
Lieut. R.A?

A.D.M.S. 2nd Div.

Report of Sanitary Officer. — April 27th 1915.

BETHUNE. Sanitary work as usual in the town. 60 men and 22 horses with drivers and carts being employed.

Work at ECOLE DE JEUNES FILLES consists of erection of new latrines, construction of new ablution benches with plumbing work for the same, and making of concrete and brick floor at a washing place in the yard.

New billets of 1st Kings Liverpools in RUE D'AIRE were inspected today. D Company billeted at 40 and 42 RUE D'AIRE appear to be overcrowded. Ditches in rear of C Company at 43 to 49 Rue D'AIRE are very foul and require cleaning out.

CIVILIAN LABOUR.
1 N.C.O. with 5 civilians employed

at billet of 170th Co R.E. (Miners) at CAMBRIN removing manure.
1 N.CO. and 12 civilians at BEUVRY working as yesterday.
17 civilians employed in BÉTHUNE and near billets of 2nd Worcesters opposite the QUAI.

BEUVRY.   1 N.CO. and 14 men employed as yesterday.
LE HAMEL. 1 N.CO and 12 men employed as yesterday.

James Clayton
Lieut. R.A.M.C.

A.D.M.S. 2nd Div.

Report of Sanitary Officer, April 28th 1915.

BETHUNE. 70 men of Garrison and Sanitary Section employed in town on sanitary work today, with 22 horses and carts.

CAMBRIN. 1 N.CO. & 5 civilians carting manure at billet of 170th Co. R.E. (Miners).

BEUVRY. 3 N.COs, 20 men + 13 civilians employed as yesterday.

LE HAMEL. 1 N.CO and 12 men as yesterday.

Billet for 1st Corps on LOCON road. Cesspit reported by Camp Commandant as urgently requiring emptying was done today by the civilian pump apparatus and 1 man and 4 civilians.

MEASLES case reported by H.Q.

4th Brigade ; . a man has been sent out tonight to carry out disinfection.

James Clayton
Lieut. RAMC

A.D.M.S. 2nd Div.
Report of Sanitary Officer. April 29th 1915.

BETHUNE. Garrison duty men, horses and carts of 2nd Divisional Train, 4th 5th and 6th Field Ambulances and of 44th Brigade Ammn. Column employed on sanitary work in the town as usual.

BEUVRY. 3 N.C.Os, 20 men and 13 civilians employed on work similar to that of yesterday.
Very good progress has been made with the manure heaps throughout the Divisional area generally. This remark applies only to those billets occupied by British troops. Large quantities of manure belonging to civilians no doubt still remain in the area. To get this manure and refuse removed, I think a new order should be issued through the civil authorities.

CAMBRIN. 1 N.C.O. 5 civilians + 2 carts removing manure from billet of 170th Co. R.E.

LE HAMEL. 1 N.C.O. and 12 men employed here.

MEASLES CASE. Officer 1st Irish Gds.

The "dug out" occupied by this Officer was disinfected last night. His billet was done today

James Clayton
Lieut. R.A.M.C.

121/5574

May 1915

Summarised reply not copied

No 11 Sanitary Officer, 2nd Division

12/5574

A.D.M.S. 2nd Division.
Report of Sanitary Officer. May 1st 1915
May 2nd & 3rd

BETHUNE.
40 men with several carts were started cleaning up the Sausage Factory and Chicory Factory in RUE DE LILLE; many loads of manure being carted away as well.

Sanitary work throughout the town and at all big billets of troops continued as normal

James Clayton
Lieut. R.A.M.C.

A.D.M.S. 2nd Div.
Report of Sanitary Officer. May 4th 1915.

BETHUNE. All the new billets of the 6th Brigade in the town have now been inspected, and where necessary, arrangements have been made for removing refuse and manure.

Sanitary work in the town continued as usual.

At the Chicory Factory RUE de LILLE, some 40 men have been employed clearing up and carting away refuse.

CAMBRIN. 1 N.C.O. and 5 civilians continue work here, removing manure and cleaning out a dirty stream.

ESSARS. 1 N.C.O. and 4 men completed work of emptying a cess pit and burying refuse.

Disinfections carried out today

at BEUVRY (billet of Lieut. IRONS 2nd H.L.I.) and at ORPHANAGE (2nd South Staffs.)

The BIVRE J. FRIES at BEUVRY will be cleaned up by a party of civilians tomorrow.

25 civilians employed today in BETHUNE and elsewhere.

James Clayton
Lieut. R.E.

A.D.M.S. 2nd Div.
Report of Sanitary Officer.   May 5th. 1915.

BETHUNE.

Refuse and manure removed from all big billets, from R.E. and 56th Battery billets, Refilling Point and from streets much used by troops eg Boulevard Victor Hugo, Place de la Republique etc. About 60 men and 12 civilians being employed in this work.

Cesspits emptied at Officers Hospital in Blvd. Victor Hugo, and 136 Rue de Lille. Several more cesspits require emptying yet. Trouble is always being experienced with the civilian contractor for this work, his work being also very slowly performed. It is most essential that I be provided with an apparatus of my own at the earliest possible moment as this work is constantly increasing.

BEUVRY. 1 N.CO. and 8 civilians employed cleaning up the École de Jeunes Filles and removing refuse from the incinerator in the square. The pump reported to me by A.D.M.S. in div. is useless for my purposes.

CAMBRIN.
1 N.CO and 7 civilians employed as yesterday.

LE HAMEL. 1 N.CO. 172 men were withdrawn from here today as they had to return to their regiments. Pumps borrowed for this work from 5th Field Co. R.E were returned to them.

34th Brigade Ammunition Column at Ferme du Roi: was inspected today by one of my N.C.Os who suggested and will carry out a proper scheme of drainage.

J. Clayton
Lieut. R.A.M.C

A.D.M.S. 2nd Div.
Report of Sanitary Officer.   May 6th 1915.

BETHUNE.
Refuse removed from all big billets
from Refilling Point, the QUAI, Rue de
l'UNIVERSITÉ. Manure removed
from M.M.P. Stables, Headquarter Stables
at HOTEL de FRANCE and SKATING
RINK in Rue de THIERS.
Special attention has also been
paid to the removal of manure
and refuse from the Sausage
Factory & Chicory Factory in
Rue de LILLE, a total of 30 men
being employed at these latter
places.   Some very dirty
ditches in the RUE du PRÉ des
SOEURS have also been cleaned
out, and the refuse removed.

Cesspits at ECOLE MICHELET were
emptied today.
The covering for latrines at the

ECOLE de JEUNES FILLES has now been completed.

BEUVRY. 1 N.C.O. and 8 civilians have now completed the cleaning of the Ecole J. Filles.

CAMBRIN. 1 NCO and 7 civilians continued work here.

26th Heavy R.G.A billet at BEUVRY

A new system of drainage is required here. 1 N.C.O. and 4 men were sent out to commence work.

James Clayton
Lieut. R.A.M.C.

A.D.M.S. 2nd Div.
Report of Sanitary Officer. May 7th 1915.

I took the Sanitary Officer 2nd London Div. over the forward area this morning to show him the type of work I have been carrying out. We visited CAMBRIN, ANNEQUIN, BEUVRY, GORRE, LE HAMEL, ESSARS and LA MOTTE.

The day's work has been as follows:
BETHUNE Removal of refuse from all my billets and Refilling Point carried out rapidly in the morning

The work at the Chicory Factory to Rue du Pré des Soeurs has been continued today by 21 civilians under 3 N.C.Os.

BEUVRY. 1 N.C.O. and 4 civilians performing drainage scheme at billet of 29th Heavy Reg. A. 100 yards of drain pipes have

114

been purchased for this work. They have also been carting away some very foul refuse &c manure. The billet hill still require a considerable expenditure of labour before it is in a proper state for habitation.

James Clayton
Burnt Stone.

A.D.M.S. 2nd Army
Report of Sanitary Officer. May 8th 1915

1. BETHUNE. All big billets in the town
cleaned up and refuse removed.
Refuse also removed from the
Boot Repairing Shop, and from the
Soldiers Pompiers near the Fire Station
Manure removed from new
Headquarters stables and from
Caserne Montmorency.
I have arranged to cart away and
burn regularly the old boots from
the Boot Shop.
Several loads of [rubble] have been
carted from RUE NEUVE to the Rue
MICHELET.
Cesspits emptied today at
RUE D'ANNEZIN and RUE BURIDAN.

REFILLING POINT I have been
unable to clean up here today
as the place was used as
a Refilling Point this morning

and afternoon.

Ditches in the Rue du Pré des
Soeurs have been cleaned out
and 20 loads of rubbish
carted away yesterday.

Francis Clayton
Lieut. R.A.M.C

A.D.M.S. 2nd Div.
Report of Sanitary Officer. May. 9th 1915.

BETHUNE.

Had a squad of 30 men at 2 a.m. at ECOLE JEUNES FILLES cleaning up in preparation for Field Ambulances. A further 30 men were brought on the work in addition at 5.30 a.m. All worked till 8.30, at which time I handed over the place to Medical Officers of both 2nd F.A. and 5th London F.A. in a clean state with all the rooms swept out, refuse burnt and removed, the yards swept up and the latrine buckets emptied.

The following billets were left in a very dirty state by the outgoing regiments last night:-

ECOLE DE JEUNES FILLES by
(2nd Inniskilling Fusiliers & 9th H.L.I.)
CASERNE MONTMORENCY by
1st Royal Berkshires.

124

These billets as well as the ORPHANAGE and TOBACCO FACTORY have all been cleaned out today.

About two thousand rounds of small arm ammunition were here collected from the above billets and returned to the Ordnance.

Sanitary work in other parts of the town, Refilling Point, continued as usual.

James Clayton

Lieut. R Some

A.D.M.S. 2nd Div.

Report of Sanitary Officer.   May 10th 1915.

BETHUNE.   All by billets in the town are now empty of troops and have been thoroughly cleaned out. Refuse and manure removed from various parts of the town and from ditches in Rue du Pré des Soeurs, and the Chicory Factory and Refilling Point.

Investigated a report by a farmer at ESSARS concerning 8 horses which have been buried on his farm. Disinfection and covering with earth is required and will be carried out tomorrow.

CASE OF DIPHTHERIA   2nd Signal Co.R.E. Disinfection of billet carried out today.

All civilian labour discharged today.

James Clayton
Lieut. R.A.M.C.

A.D.M.S. 2nd Div.

Report of Sanitary Officer. May 11th 1915

BETHUNE — Sanitary work in the town, at all by billets and Refilling Point was continued today as usual.

Cesspits at No 6. Field Ambulance emptied today.

Refuse removed from Rue du Pré des boeufs.

16 loads of manure carted away from Salvage Factory.

Several loads of shale carted from ANNEZIN to the ORPHANAGE.

All the by billets in BETHUNE were occupied today by troops of the 7th ov Late Divisions

LACOUTURE — 1 N.CO and 12 men sent out for sanitary work.

at Advanced 2nd Div. Reporting Centre.

BEUVRY 2 N.COs and 12 men worked at drainage scheme at billet of 20th Heavy R.G.A.

ESSARS. 1 NCO and 6 men carried out covering up of 8 horses partly buried in fields.

A.D.M.S. — 2nd Div.
Report of Sanitary Officer 19 my 12th 1915

Knocked off work in BÉTHUNE
and removed sanitary section
to LOCON.

J. Clayton
Lieut. R.A.M.C.

A.D.M.S. 2nd Div.

Report of Sanitary Officer. May 13th 1915

Sanitary Section cleaned up & arranged new billet in LOCON.

LA COUTURE. 14 men and 2 N.C.Os sent out to LA COUTURE to commence work of cleaning up in the village.

Sanitary Section stores brought in from BETHUNE, and sanitary work commenced in LOCON.

J Compton
Lieut. R.A.M.C.

A.D.M.S. 2nd Div.
Report of Sanitary Officer May 14th.

LOCON. Work of cleaning up in the village continued.
Rotary brush fetched from GORRE and started in LOCON.
4 horses & drivers obtained from 3rd & 2nd F.A. These were sent to BETHUNE to bring out 4 carts and remainder of Sanitary Section Stores to LOCON.

LACOUTURE. 1 N.C.O. + 4 men continued work here today.

One N.C.O. sent to RICHEBOURG and one to LE TOURET to inspect the areas occupied by 5th and 6th Brigades and report to me.

Garrison duty section arrived this morning from BETHUNE

Fatigue parties were drawn
from it for work in LOCON.

TUBS for collecting rain water.

I have about 10 of these
ready + scrubbed out.

J. Clayton
Lieut. R??ne

A. D. M. S. 2nd Divn

Report of Sanitary Officer. May 15th 1915.

LILLERS. Party of 1 N.C.O. and 12 men
at work in village, cleaning
up ditches etc. They also cleaned
out 4 open wells.
Carpenters and plumbers of Sanitary
Section at work preparing index
boards for marking the chief
sources of water supply in the
village.

LA COUTURE, RICHEBOURG, and
LE TOURET.
2 N.C.Os & 20 men
with implements and 1 cart were
sent to each of the above places
for sanitary work in the
villages. Some of the
surroundings of billets in these
places are in a very bad
state.

I have visited these parties
today to direct their work.

3 barrels for water, sent out
to A.D.M.S. reserve and 2nd Div.

J. Clayton
Lieut. R.A.M.C.

A.D.M.S. 2nd Div.
Report of Sanitary Officer. May 23rd.

LABEUVRIERE.

Fatigue party of 80 men worked today in cleaning up ditches and refuse in the village, three carts and horses being also employed.

Cess pit at billet of Section No 4 F.A. in this village was emptied today.

The problem of dealing with manure in middens in the area now occupied by the 2nd Div. does not seem to have been tackled previously. Can Units of the 2nd Div. be asked through Routine Orders to deal with the middens in their billets immediately.

J. Clayton
Lieut. RAM

A.D.M.S. 2nd Div.

Report of Sanitary Officer.   May 24th

LABEUVRIERE.

Sanitary Section and 50 men of fatigue party, 5 horses & drivers, with 3 carts and cesspit apparatus were engaged today in LABEUVRIERE emptying cesspits, and removing manure and filth from ditches. Deep pits in a field are being dug to receive these matters.

As the removal of manure, refuse ditch cleanings etc is certain to be a work which will have to be carried out continuously by the sanitary section throughout the whole of the campaign both summer and winter, would it not be possible to provide the sanitary section with say, 3 tip carts (scotch carts) and 3 horses and drivers of its own. As many as 14 and 16 carts have been employed at one time by me; 3 carts would therefore be the minimum required.

At present carts of all sorts and sizes have to be requisitioned, borrowed, hired or stolen in order to get the work done, and horses and drivers have to be obtained from various units — the Divisional Train, Field Ambulances, R.E., Divisional Mounted Troops, Ammunition Columns, and from civilians — all under different circumstances and special conditions, whilst great difficulty is experienced as regards the harness.

These complications are both very worrying and very detrimental to the smooth and efficient

working of the whole system.
I should greatly appreciate
having horses, carts and drivers
under my own control, and
could certainly work 3' of each
continuously.

James Clayton
Lieut, R&me.

A.D.M.S. 2nd Division
Report of Sanitary Officer.   May 25th
1915

LABEUVRIERE.

WATER SUPPLY.   All the chief sources of water in the village have now been marked with boards showing where water may be obtained and roughly the quality of the water. Two pumps have also been repaired.

Work of spraying manure heaps, removing liquid and manure from the middens of billets, cleaning of ditches and drains has been proceeded with.
For this work about 30 men with 4 carts & horses have been employed.
A further 20 men were engaged today in digging a deep pit for the reception of the contents of cesspits.

James Clayton
Lieut R.A.M.C.

A.D.M.S. 2nd Div.

Report of Sanitary Officer. May 26, 27, 28th, 1915

Sanitary work in LABEUVRIERE continued with men of Sanitary Sections and fatigue party.

1 large Destructor for refuse has been built.

Manure has been removed from several farm billets & from the Forge in the square and the 2nd Divisional Train.

Pump and Tank Cart have emptied several dirty ditches and removed liquid manure from cesspits of farm billets.

Case of measles (PTE THOMAS, 2nd Worcesters) at ECQUEDECQUES. Disinfection of billet carried out on 28/2.

J Clayton
Lieut. RAMC

A.D.M.S 2nd Div.
Report of Sanitary Officer. May 16th, 1915

LOCON. Work on roads, ditches etc
carried on in Locon with 80 men
from Garrison duty section and
4 horses & carts from Divn Train.

Have arranged a scheme for
marking the principal sources
for obtaining water in the district.
The immediate area round and
in Locon has been systematically
surveyed for all wells & pumps.

Motor lorry sent out during the
day to collect wounded from
Advanced Dressing Stations in
the Richebourg - Lacouture area.
55 men were evacuated in
3 journeys to Bethune.

7 p.m. I reported to O.C. 6th
Field Ambulance BETHUNE

and carried out ANTITETANIC inoculation.

J Clayton
Lieut. RAMC

A.D.M.S. 2nd Div.

Report of Sanitary Officer. May 17th 1915

LOZON. Work carried on as yesterday with 40 men of fatigue party.

Motor lorry turned out at 10 p.m. on 16th for evacuation of wounded, and again at 2 p.m. on 17th.

J. Clayton
Lieut. R.A.M.C.

A.D.M.S. 2nd Div
Report of Sanitary Officer May 18th

LOCON. Sanitary work with fatigue party continued. Received 1 tank cart and suction pump from D.A.D.O.S. 2nd Div.

Motor lorry turned out in afternoon at 2pm and worked all night with a party of 12 men from Sanitary Section evacuating wounded from Advanced Dressing Station at RICHEBOURG.

I reported as ordered by you to O.C. 4th F.A. at BETHUNE at 10pm and worked till 8 am next morning.

J Clayton
Lieut R.A.M.C.

A.D.M.S. 2nd Div.

Report of Sanitary Officer. May 19th

Sanitary work with N.C.O.s & men of sanitary section and fatigue party carried on in LOCON and surrounding district.

J Clayton
Lieut: R.A.M.C.

A.D.M.S. 2nd Div.

Report of Sanitary Officer. May 20. 16

Removed Sanitary Section and part of stores to LABEUVRIERE. Section settled in new billet and work commenced on cleaning up village.

J. Clayton
Lieut. RAMC

A.D.M.S. 2nd Div.
Report of Sanitary Officer May 29th

LABRUVRIERE.

Fatigue party of 120 men worked under supervision of N.C.Os of Sanitary Section in cleaning up village ditches etc, digging latrines, refuse pits and so on. Remainder of stores brought from town

J Clayton
Lieut. R.A.M.C

A.D.M.S. 2nd Div.
Report of Sanitary Officer 14 May 2000

LABEUVRIERE.

150 men of fatigue party continued work in village in the morning but had to stop to get sanitary section & stores removed to a new billet, as old billet was taken over by No 4. F.A.

Have arranged for requisition carts from the Maire and horses from the HQ Company of Divisional Train.

J. Clayton
Lieut. R.A.M.C.

A.D.M.S. 2nd Divn.
Report of Sanitary Officer. May 29th 30th

LABEUVRIÈRE

Sanitary Section men, 25 fatigue party, 4 carts, removing manure from behind Forge and Motor Machine Gun Section's billet.

Pump & tank cart removing fluid from middens & pools / at above billet.

Ditches cleaned & refuse removed

J. Clayton
Lieut R.A.M.C.

A.D.M.S. 2nd Div.
Report of Sanitary Officer. May 31st
LAPEUVRIERE

Sanitary Section men, 28 fatigue
party, 2 carts removing manure
and refuse as yesterday;
packing stores. cleaning pump
and tank cart & implements
filling in trench and covering
refuse with earth.
Fatigue party sent to LAPUGNOY to
relieve of vegetation guards.
Clayton
Lieut R.A.M.C.

12/6/15

June 1915

Summarised but not copied
2nd Division

No 11 Sainthugleston. 2nd Division

Vol VI

13/6/15

Ans

War Diary.

O.C. Sanitary Section

2nd Division.

June 1915

A.D.M.S. 2nd Division
Report of Sanitary Officer for week
June 1st to 7th.

June 1st
Went to NOEUX LES MINES to organise
sanitary work for the 4th Brigade in
that town.
Sent Pump + Tank Cart with N.C.O and
men to empty cesspit at 5th
Field Ambulance at NOEUX LES
MINES on receipt of urgent
request from O.C. 5 of A.
Removed 23 Latrine buckets from
ORPHANAGE at BETHUNE and
handed them over to 4th Guards
Brigade.
Tried to obtain assistance from
municipal authorities to
help clean of the place as
it was in a very dirty state.

June 2nd. 4 N.C.Os + 18 men
with implements sent to
NOEUX LES MINES for sanitary

work. Palliettes by 4th Brigade; returned by 5th F.A.

Purchased 16 more Latrine buckets + sent these with a further 27 and 20 tubs to 4th Brigade.
Total handed over to 4th Brigade –
   66 Latrine buckets
   20 Tubs (for washing)
   1 Rotary Brush (from Ponts et Chaussees, BETHUNE)

Removed Sanitary Section + all remainder of Stores from LABEUVRIERE to GOSNAY.

June 2nd   Started sanitary section cleaning up billets and village of GOSNAY.
Went to LES TREBIS on request of 6th Brigade to organise Sanitary work in that town, and to 5th Brigade at GAZINGARBE

June 4th   20 with implements
2 NCOs and 20 men, sent to
LES BREBIS for Sanitary work
with 6th Brigade ; 1 N.CO. and
10 men sent with implements
to 5th Brigade at MAZINGARBE.

June 5th   Went to HOUCHIN to
organise Sanitation of 7th
Mountain Battery. Sent out
1 NCO and 5 men to help
them do this work.

Distribution of Sanitary Section
therefore is :—

NOEUX LES MINES.
  4 NCOs and 4 men of Sanitary Sec.
  20 men of Convalescent Company

LES BREBIS:
  2 NCOs and 2 men of Sana Sec
  18 men of Convalescent Co

MAZINGARBE
    1 N.C.O. + 1 man of San. Sect.
        9 men of Convalescent Co.
HOUCHIN.
    1 N.C.O. of San. det.
    5 men of Convalescent Co.
GONNAY
    The rest of Sanitary Section
    and some 12 men of
    Convalescent Company

Work proceeding at all the above
places, all of them being
visited by myself & my
Staff Sergeant every day.
Implements necessary
supplied to these working
parties every day.
Disinfection place of German
wounded carried out today
at CORONS, near VERMELLES.

June 6th.
Area occupied by 2nd Division
changed today.
Party from LES BREBIS recalled.

June 7th
Sanitary parties from
NOEUX LES MINES and
MAZINGARBE brought back.

Cneho [?] wounded 17. men. Draft [?]
carried out at NOEUX LES MINES
K I.A. to in hosp.

James Clayton
Lieut. R.A.M.C.

52

A.D.M.S. Meadow

Report of Sanitary Officer

June 8th.

Organised sanitary work at GOMMECOURT and HEBUTERNE. Pump and tank cart used for emptying cesspits & middens every day.

Went to MOYENNEVILLE on request of 6th Brigade to organise work of cleaning up the place which is in a filthy condition.

Also went to Advanced H.Q. 2nd Divn at SAULTY CHATEAUVERT to organise sanitary work there.

June 9th

6 N.C.Os and 26 men (with officer) sent to 6th Brigade at MOYENNEVILLE. 2 N.C.Os and 12 men sent

54

with implements to SAILLY
LABOURSE.

Two civilian cases of typhoid
investigated at LAPUGNOY.

June 10th

Work proceeding at VIMY, LES,
Advanced 2nd Div, SAILLY
LABOURSE, GOSNAY, HESDIGNEUL
under constant supervision.
Implements necessary, stock
of disinfectants, paraffin
bleaching powder etc issued
out to these working parties
every day.
MOTOR LORRY sent to repair
workshops at LAPUGNOY for
overhaul. Arranged for
temporary loan of one G.S. wagon
from Divisional train.

James Clayton
Lieut R.A.M.C.

A.D.M.S. 2nd Div.

Report of Sanitary Officer. June 11th.
Visited Advanced med Dw, SAILLY
LABOURSE, and NOYELLES to see Sanitary
parties at work.

Also went to VERMELLES by
arrangement with M.O. 36th Brig.
R.F.A. to note the Sanitary state
of that place and to advise
on burial of bodies. This place
also is infested with flies & bluebottles.
Have arranged to send out an
N.C.O. with men & a stock of
quicklime & chloride of lime for
reburial of dead bodies.

GOSNAY, HESDIGNEUL. Work of
removing manure, ditch cleaning
etc proceeding as usual. Also
started work of cleaning streets
as per 1st Corps Order

J. Clayton
Lieut R.A.M.C.

A.D.M.S. 2nd Div.
Report of Sanitary Officer. June 12th 1915.

Went to LAPUGNOY to investigate cases of Enteric amongst civilians. Recent cases of Enteric in 1st Irish Guards & 2nd Coldstream Gds. are probably traceable to residence in this village. Houses have been placed out of bounds, and most of the water taps & pumps labelled with a warning notice.

June 13th

Inspected billets of 2nd South Staffs. at VERQUINEUL. Much manure remains in middens which ought to be got away by Units in occupation of billets.
Sanitary Parties set to work at NOYELLES, SAILLY LABOURSE, SAINS and HERSIN NEUIL as yesterday.

J. Clayton
Lieut. R.A.M.C.

A.D.M.S. 2nd Div.

Report of Sanitary Officer. June 14th

Sent out Sanitary party of 1 N.C.O. and 4 men to VERMELLES with a stock of quicklime and chloride of lime for treatment of partially buried bodies.

Redistribution of Sanitary Section is therefore at present.

Place	S.S.	Consold. Co.
At Corps H.Q.	1 N.C.O.	
VERMELLES	1 N.C.O.	4 men
NOYELLES	3 N.C.Os / 4 men	15 men
Advanced 2nd Div.	1 N.C.O.	2 men
H.Q. 2nd Div.	L.Cpl. Tulley	3 men
SAILLY LABOURSE	1 N.C.O / 1 man	9 men
VERQUIN	1 N.C.O. / 2 men	6 men
GOSNAY and HESDIGNEUL	6 N.C.Os / 7 men	2 N.C.Os / 13 men

A.D.M.S. 2nd Div.
Report of Sanitary Officer. June 15th 1915

Sanitary Parties at work as yesterday
at VERMELLES, NOYELLES, SAILLY
LABOURSE, GUINAY & HESDIGNEUL.

With D.A.D.M.S. inspected all billets
of 2nd D.A.C. at HESDIGNEUL.
Arranged for working party to be sent
out tomorrow, with implements,
paraffin, & tubs for sterilised drinking
water.

J Clayton
Lieut. RAMC

A.D.M.S. 2nd Div.
Report of Sanitary Officer. June 16th.

Visited FOUQUEREUIL (6th Brigade changed with 5th last night) to arrange for working sanitary parties at FOUQUEREUIL, VERQUIN, VERQUINEUL and LAPOURTE.

Visited sanitary parties at NOYELLES, SAILLY LABOURSE, & Advanced 2nd Div. Several days work still remains at these places.

Arranged for further work at H.Q. 2nd Div. Train, 2nd D.A.C. at HESDIGNEUL.

J. Clayton
Lieut. R.A.M.C.

A.D.M.S. 2nd Div
Report of Sanitary Officer. June 17th 1915

Sanitary parties continued work at NOYELLES, VERMELLES & AILLY LABOURSE, and GOSNAY. The work of sweeping the roads in GOSNAY has been taken on by sanitary section and men of Convalescent Company, as these roads are much used by horses and are covered with manure and dust. Special work in HESDIGNEUL consisted of removal of manure and refuse from a large heap at H.Q. 2nd Div. Train, and cleaning out a ditch at No. 3 Section 2nd D.A.C.

J Clayton
Lieut. R.A.M.C.

A.D.M.S. 2nd Div.
Report of Sanitary Officer.   June 18th 1915

Went to AMIENS to purchase two more spraying pumps for spraying manure & for small garden syringes for spraying solution for fly-killing in the trenches.

Work carried on as yesterday at VERMELLES, NOYELLES, SAILLY LABOURSE, VERQUINEUL, GOSNAY and HESDIGNEUL.

4 wooden covers for a new type of trench latrine were made.

James Clayton
Lieut. R.A.M.C.

A.D.M.S. 2nd Div.
Report of Sanitary Officer. June 19th

Carried out disinfection of billet at CAMBRIN of 3 cases of diptheria from 1st Herts Regt.

Work carried on as yesterday at VERMELLES, NOYELLES, SAILLY LABOURSE, GONAY and VERDIG- NEUL. Flies and disinfectant sent out to these parties nearly every day.

J. Clayton
Lieut. R.A.M.C.

A.D.M.S. 2nd Div.
Report of Sanitary Officer. June 20th
I visited today the working parties
at NOYELLES, SAILLY LABOURSE
LABOURSE, and the Advanced 2nd
Div.
The work of getting the place
clean and of removing manure
and emptying pits at NOYELLES
should now be completed in
about 2 days' time, after
which I propose to remove the
party for work at BEUVRY and
VERQUINEUL.
At the latter place there are
large amounts of manure in
middens to be covered over
or removed. There is also
several days' work (possibly
some weeks' work) for the
pump and tank cart at SAILLY
LABOURSE, and this work
becomes urgent.
At NOYELLES there is one

74

casualty of the Sanitary Section to report — Pte. CLIFTON, shrapnel wound in right hand and chin evacuated from 5th F.A. today.

Work at SAILLY LABOURSE, VERMELLES, GUINAY and HESDIGNEUL proceeding as yesterday.

J Clayton.
Lieut. R.A.M.C.

A.D.M.S. 2nd Div

Report of Sanitary Officer. June 21st.

I visited SAILLY LABOURSE this morning and inspected the work of the sanitary parties at Advanced 2nd Div. and in the village. Six more men and 1 N.CO. were sent out to SAILLY LABOURSE this morning to help with the work there and at LABOURSE.

The parties working away from my headquarters are therefore now:

    VERMELLES   1 N.CO. + 4 men
    NOYELLES   4 N.COs. 25 men
                            2 horses.
    SAILLY LABOURSE   3 N.COs. 18 men

I propose to remove the party at NOYELLES on Wednesday morning (23rd inst.) as by that time they will have completed the work for which they were sent out, and

78

there is very urgent work for them to do in SAILLY LABOURSE, VERQUINEUL and elsewhere. I have made all the arrangements for their removal and transference to other places.

I also visited this morning the 4th Brigade & 6th Brigade Headquarters at ANNEQUIN to arrange for sanitary work to be done in that area.

P. Clayton
Lieut. R.A.M.C.

A.D.M.S. 2nd Div.

Report of Sanitary Officer.   June 22nd 1915.

Inspected parts of 5th Brigade trenches. These are on the whole kept very clean, but they swarm with bluebottles. Some of the old dugouts in old French communication trenches have been fouled by their use as latrines, but considering the enormous length of these communication trenches they are ~~not~~ really satisfactory.

The large number of bluebottles points to exposed decomposing flesh. Attention might be called to the necessity for burying all exposed flesh, even the bodies of field mice and moles.

I would strongly recommend the provision of about 30 more syringes for spraying parts of the trenches with weak cresol solution.

82

Six more wooden latrine covers will be made and forwarded to the M.O. of Units in the trenches.

I should like your opinion on the following points:—

i. Latrines at intervals along the communication trenches
ii. Filling in old dugouts in old communication trenches
iii. The provision of sanitary police for the trenches, say 1 man per battalion drawn from the Convalescent Company

J Clayton
Lieut. R.A.M.C.

A.D.M.S. 2nd Div.

Sanitary Party at NOETELLES were withdrawn today, and Pump & Tank Cart sent to SAILLY LABOURSE.

Distribution of Sanitary Sections & Corps. Co. today:—

Place	S.S.	Corps Co.
1st Corps H.Q.	1 N.C.O.	
VERMELLES	1 N.C.O	4 men
SAILLY LABOURSE	3 N.C.Os. 4 men	1 N.C.O. 21 men
Advanced 2nd Div.	1 N.C.O.	2 men
2nd Div. H.Q.	L. Cpl. Elsey	3 men
GOSNAY and HESDIGNEUL	8 N.C.Os. 2 M.T. RSC 9 men	5 N.C.Os. 40 men

I have arranged with both Brigades to send to ANNEQUIN tomorrow, 3 N.C.Os and 12 men with implements.

J. Clayton
Lieut. R.A.M.C.

23/6/15

A.D.M.S. 2nd Div.

Report of Sanitary Officer. June 24th

Inspected sanitary party's work at BAILEUL LABOURSE today. The field by Advanced 2nd Div. and As Transport Lines by Irish Guards & Grenadier Guards should be better looked after. The latrines were unsatisfactory, paper being littered along the hedge.

Sanitary party of 3 N.C.Os and 12 men sent out to 6th Brigade at ANNEQUIN today.

J. Clayton
Lieut. RAMC

3 wooden latrine covers of new type have been sent to N.Os 2nd Grenadier Gds. 1st KRR. and 2nd Inniskilling F.

A.D.M.S. 2nd Div.

Removed Sanitary section from GONAY to VAUDRICOURT.
Sanitary party withdrawn from VERQUIN
Present distribution of sanitary section & Conv. Co. —

	F.A.	Conv. Co.
1st Corps H.Q.	1 N.C.O.	
SAILLY LABOURSE	{ 2 N.C.O. { 6 men	1 N.C.O. 13 men
LAPUGNOY and VERQUINEUL	1 N.C.O.	8 men
ANNEQUIN and CAMBRIN	2 N.C.O. 1 man	1 N.C.O. 10 men
Advanced 2nd Div.	1 N.C.O.	2 men
2nd Div. H.Q. VAUDRICOURT	L/Cpl Elman Remainder of Sanitary Section and Conv. Co.	10 men

J. Clayton
Lieut, R.A.M.C.

25.6.15.

A.D.M.S. 2nd Div
June 27th 1915

Sanitary parts withdrawn from
SAILLY LABOURSE and SAILLEURSE.
Two lorry loads of stores and
implements removed from
VAUDRICOURT to BETHUNE.

Materials for construction of
incinerator for burning excreta
were brought in BETHUNE.

J Clayton
Lieut. R.A.M.C.

A.D.M.S. 2nd Div.
May 29th

Bought 15 more syringes in
BOULOGNE this morning.

Sanitary Section removed from
VAUDRICOURT to BETHUNE.

I have organised carts, horses
and men to commence
work tomorrow.

Your notes re billets at
OBLINGHEM noted.

J Clayton
Lieut RAMC

N.D.M.S. 2nd Div.

Report of Sanitary Officer. June 29th 18

BETHUNE

Several places in the town have been left in a very dirty condition by the outgoing Division — particularly the ECOLE DE GARÇONS at the PLACE DE LILLE, the school in the RUE LOUIS BLANC, whilst there are large accumulations of refuse in various billets.

The cesspits in the town are quite full and require emptying immediately. There is also urgent work for my tank cart at ORLINGHEM, ANNEQUIN and elsewhere so that I could really do with two such apparatuses.

I should be glad of the help for a week or so of an officer to attend to the Sanitary work of the area outside

BETHUNE as there is enough work in the Town itself to claim the whole of my attention for about a week until the sanitation of the place has got into a satisfactory working order.

James Clayton
Lieut. R.E.

A.D.M.S. 2nd Div.

Report of Sanitary Officer.   June 24th 1915

Organised sanitary work in
BETHUNE at present with 8 lp
carts and 1 large waggon;
employing 4 horses of H.Q. Co. 2nd
F.A. Third and 8 of No. 6. F.A.
Between 40 and 50 men from
Conv. Co. employed removing
refuse and manure in various
billets.

Cesspits emptied at 36 Rue D'
Arnezin and at Case De
Garcons.

A sanitary party of 1 N.C.O. and 1
man of that dept. and 10 men of
Conv. Co. were sent for work at
OBLINGHEM. They are billeted
+ rationed by No 4 F.A. at
VENDIN.

Work of building incinerator

by Tobacco factory for
combustion of excreta was
commenced to-day.

J Clayton
Lieut R.A.M.C.

121/6210

S   2nd Division
    Summoned but not acted

July 1915.

187/6210

Mr N. Sany. Lector

Not Set

ans

Latrine buckets + seats sent
to 5th F.A. at VENDIN

31.7.15   J.O Sherwood
                8th R.A.M.C.

A.D.M.S 2nd Div

Sanitary officer's Report

Refuse removed from all areas as usual

Ditch work at St Quesnoy proceeding

Work of cleaning the Chicory factory at St Quesnoy proceeding.

Waterpipe at Caserne Montmorency repaired

Latrine buckets at Tobacco factory cleaned & returned to store. Work on same at Ecole de Jeune filles proceeding.

Bricks for incinerator at 1st King's Rifles provided

- ADMS II Div

Sanitary Officer's Report

Refuse removed from all areas as usual.

Work on ditches at G. Quarry proceeding.

Work on incinerator at 3rd Cay ASC commenced.

Latrine seats fixed at Church Rue d'Aire

Grease traps at Tobacco Factory now completed

Work on Ablution benches at Orphanage proceeding.

30/7/15 F.O. Sherwood
          S.O.   Lt. RAMC

Work on ablution benches at
Church at Rue d'Isere proceeding.

All billets reported left clean
by outgoing troops.

J.E. Thompson
Lt.?. A.M?

29/7/15

ADMS - II Div.

Removal of refuse & manure from all billets & areas.

Removal of manure from Champ de Mars & rue [?]

Work of filling drain [?] at École [?] Communicated.

Work of creating [?] latrines at billets of 7 [?] Company Communicated.

Multiplying [?] of waste paper at École de [?] Communicated.

Materials for incinerators & latrines [?] at billets of 31st Coy A.S.C. prepared.

47

A.D.M.S. II Div.

Report of Sanitary Officer

Removal of refuse manure &c from all dugouts carried out as usual.

New incinerator at Ravine Monténégro completed.

Building of Echelon washhouse at Chemin Rue Dame progressing.

Pumps at & bathing huts repaired.

Preparation of ground troops at Tobacco factory progressing.

G D Shannon
Lt R.A.M.C.

28.7.15

A.D.M.S. II Div

Report of Sanitary Officer

Removal & disposal of refuse from all Coys & Billets in hand.

Removal of manure from Claury d.O.H area is progressing.

Inspected all the billets in Werkin area. Ablution benches by process of erection at Church st.
Preparation of grease trap at Tobacco Factory in progress.

Ground at Tobacco Factory is being prepared for erection of ablution benches.

Cesspits emptied at Ecole des Jeunes Filles & at 29 Rue Porcelet

27.1.15   G.D Sherwood Lt R.A.M.C

A.D.M.S. 2nd Div.
Report of Sanitary Officer. July 26th/15

BETHUNE

Removal of refuse from
all by billets as usual.
Commenced removal of manure
from Champ de Mars into the
deep pit there.
Made arrangements for erecting a
better collection place at the
Tobacco Factory than the existing
one.
Employed Rotary Brush sweeping
up certain streets and the
yard of the Skating Rink.
Komp and Tomb Cart emptied
cesspit at G.S. Office and
another in Rue du College.
Manure removed daily from H.Q.
Stables and from stables of
Military Police.

J. Clayton
Lieut. R.A.M.C.

from Rue du Pre des Soeurs

Mr Queens Cipt Tilman factory
and 2 or 3 [unreadable] families
the Ecole de Jeunes Filles
(25.7.4) [unreadable] in [unreadable]

J. Clayton
Lieut RAMC

A.D.M.S. 2nd Div.

Report of Sanitary Officer. July 24th and 25th

BETHUNE.

Removal of refuse from all billets as usual.

Continued work on Ablution Benches at ORPHANAGE and SKATING RINK.

Made arrangements for ablution benches at ECOLE PAUPERT and ECOLE LIBRE.

Provided timber for 9 wooden Latrine Covers each for M.Gs. 1st Herts, 5th Kings and 3rd Coldstream Gds.

Two parties of men Cleaning up Refuse Tip and Manure Tip.

20 loads Manure removed from Champ de Mars.
Cesspits emptied at TOBACCO FACTORY
Large heaps of refuse removed

Recreation Room, Ecole
Michelet, 20 Quai
Marché aux Chevaux.

Notified Germans [?] Authorities
about removal of refuse in
the Rue du Pré des Sœurs
and of the "cabinets" round
the Canal Basin in front du
Rû (36th Brigade R.E.A.)

J. Clayton
Lieut. R.Somes[?]

A.D.M.S. 2nd Div.
Report of Sanitary Officer.   July 7th to 13th '15

BÉTHUNE.   Sanitary work continued
throughout the town and at all
by billets.
2 N.C.O + 20 men employed
removing town manure
refuse at No 6 F.A. Transport by
the Marché aux Chevaux.
Continued construction of
ablution places and drainage
system for yard at ORPHANAGE.

Manure being gradually
removed from Champ de
Mars.
Purchased cement and wood
for construction of several
ablution places in billets
in the town, and wood for
mule latrine covers.
Cesspits completed at

A.E.4...
Офс. Sanitary Officer.   July 21st /15

BETHUNE

5th Brigade vacated all billets in BETHUNE and left them very satisfactory except the house occupied by M.G. Section and Transport of 19th H.L.I. which was only in fair condition.

Sanitary Party, pump & truck cart withdrawn today from 6th Brigade H.Q.

This party has completed the cleaning up as far as possible of the LE PREOL, LE QUESNOY and RUE FIXE areas, and liquid manure middens have also been emptied in the LE PREOL and LE QUESNOY districts.

J Clayton
Lieut. R.A.M.C.

clean up ground by Rev. GERCHER's
coffee stall and to start all
the necessary sanitary arrangements
This was satisfactorily completed
on the 20th inst.

Made arrangements with 6th
Inf Brigade to withdraw tomorrow
the whole of the sanitary party
attached to them.

Motor lorry sent to Repair
Workshops for general overhaul.

J. Clayton
Lieut RAMC.

A.D.M.S. 2nd Div

Report of Sanitary Officer.   July 19th & 20th

BETHUNE.   Inspected all billets in
            Western part of BETHUNE. There are
            still accommodations for men
            on Champ de Mars to be removed.

            Made arrangements for provision
            of a supply of large barrels for
            holding cresol solutions and of
150   tubs/basins for use of troops
            in the big billets.
            Dirty & choked drain at Skating
            Rink cleaned out and
            completed erection of ablution
            bench and repair to water
            pump.
            Several new incinerators built
            in various parts of the town.

            Sanitary party of 1 N.C.O. and
            10 men sent to ANNEQUIN to

24

Report of Sanitary Officer July 18th – 1915

BETHUNE. Sanitary work in the town continued as normal.

J Clayton
Lieut. RAMC

Report of A.D.M.S. Sanitary Officer. July 17th 1915.

BÉTHUNE — Sanitary work throughout the town and at all big billets as usual.

Incinerator for Secreta opened today and worked satisfactorily.

Party of 1 N.C.O. and 13 men with pump & tank cart sent out to reinforce the Sanitary Party attached to 6th Inf. Brigade.

J. Clayton
Lieut. R.A.M.C.

emptied at No 57. A. VENDIN.
On 16th, 2 cesspits at 70th
(H.)Battery R.G.A. near ANNEQUIN
were emptied.

J. Clayton
Lieut R.A.M.C.

A.D.M.S. 2nd Div.
Report of Sanitary Officer July 15th & 16th

BETHUNE. Refuse & manure removed from all billets in the town and many roads in the town swept up with Rotary Brush & sweepings removed. The Municipal Authorities are also doing more in this respect & so that the streets are now much cleaner than they have been before. Two extra horses from 2nd Div. Train with drivers, are lent every day to the Town authorities.

New Ablution Bench at ORPHANAGE
This work has now been commenced and is well under way. Also one at the Skating Rink.

Cesspits.
On 15th, 3 cesspits

A.D.M.S. 2nd Div.

Report of Sanitary Officer. July 14th

BETHUNE. Sanitary work, removal
of refuse & manure as usual.

Cesspits emptied at
   R.A. Headquarters
   24, Marché aux Chevaux
   École de GARÇONS

Limewashing walls of latrines
in [billets] in BETHUNE.

New ablution bench started
at SKATING RINK.

J Crompton
Lieut, R.A.M.C

A.D.M.S. 2nd Division July 13th
Report of Sanitary Officer.

BETHUNE Sanitary work continued

6th Brigade handed over billets in BETHUNE to 5th Brigade. All in satisfactory condition
Commenced cleaning ditch by 6th Brigade H.Q. in Faubourg St. PRY.

Sanitary Party at 5th Brigade H.Q. on Canal started work in area Pont Fixe and from Windy Corner back towards Canal.

12 Horses buried by fatigue party of Gunners working under direction of Sanitary Corporal in area of BELLENVUE Wood.

J. Clayton
Lieut. RAMC

A.D.M.S. 2nd Div.
Report of Sanitary Officer. July 12th 1915

BETHUNE.
Large incinerator by Tobacco factory practically completed.
Refuse & Manure removed as usual from all big billets.

40 Latrine Buckets sent to Irish Gds. for use at BEUVRY.

New seats ordered for latrines at ORPHANAGE.
Commenced to limewash all the walls of latrines in BETHUNE.
Started new ablution place at ORPHANAGE. This will take a week or so to complete.

J. Clayton
Lieut. RAMC

A.D.M.S. 2nd Division.
Report of Sanitary Officer. July 10th 1915

BÉTHUNE. Have made arrangements for 2 horses daily, morning and afternoon from the 2nd Div. Train for use with 2 extra carts which the Maire is willing to employ in the cleansing of the streets.

Sanitary work in the town continued as usual.
Finished emptying cesspit at No 6. 7.A.

Visited 5th Inf. Brigade HQ this afternoon and arranged for reburial of 12 horses of R.F.A. about which a complaint was recently received by the 2nd Div.

J. Clayton
Lieut. R.A.M.C.

A.D.M.S. 2nd Division

Report of Sanitary Officer.   July 9th 1915.

BETHUNE.   Sanitary work continued.
Latrines all moved at ORPHANAGE
to new position in neighbouring
field.
Work proceeding on large incinerator
by Tobacco Factory.
Cesspit at No 6 Field Ambulance
(COLLEGE ST. VAAST) emptied today.
Total number of NCOs & men
employed in BETHUNE — 99.

J Clayton
Lieut. RAMC

A.D.M.S. 2nd Div
Report of Sanitary Officer. July 8th 1915.

BETHUNE.   Sanitary work continued.
Cesspits emptied at ECOLE
SEVIGNE and at 121 Rue de LILLE.

With A.D.M.S 37th Divn inspected
all the principal billets in
BETHUNE.

J. Clayton
Lieut. R.A.M.C

A.D.M.S. 2nd Div.

Report of Sanitary Officer July 7th 1915

BETHUNE. Sanitary work continued. Cesspits emptied at ECOLE LIBRE and at 136 Rue de LILLE

Work of Sanitary Party with 5th Inf. Brigade at LE PREOL and LE QUESNOY proceeding satisfactorily.
My N.C.O. in charge of this party stated that when he arrived at H.Q. 5th Inf. Brigade he could find no provision for the proper and regular construction of Latrines for the men attached to the Headquarters. Can I be informed please whether there is any R.A.M.C. personnel attached to H.Q. of Brigades.

J. Clayton
Lieut. R.A.M.C.

inf. Brigades; Remainder
all working in and around
BETHUNE.

James Clayton
Lieut. R&me

A.D.M.S 2nd Division
Report of Sanitary Officer.   Feby. 6th 1915.

BETHUNE   Sanitary work in Town and at all billets continued as usual. Cesspit emptied at École JULES FERRY. All units in BETHUNE who have horses have been notified of the position of manure tips and that they should cart their manure there.

SCARLET FEVER case.   Billet of 1 Officer 1st Kings at 11 Rue Chateau de l'Eau disinfected today.

All Units of 6th Brigade who took over billets from the 4th Bgd in BETHUNE have been notified of the states of their billets.

Present distribution of San. Sect. & Corps Cor. Co:—

2 N.C.Os and 13 men at 5th

Report of Liaison Officer, July 19th

BETHUNE. Enemy work on the
streets of the town continues
as yesterday.
One more successful completed operation
JULES FERRY.
Explosions have occurred in the
following places during 1 week:—
   TOBACCO FACTORY   1
   OR PITCHARD ?   1
   ECOLE MICHELET   1
   ECOLE DE GARCONS   1
   40 Rue D'ARRAS   1
   36 Rue D ???   1
   ECOLE JULES FERRY   2

4th Guards Brigade OP killed
in BETHUNE today but in
inspecting conditions.

/ Clayton
Lieut. ???

Report of Sanitation [illegible date]

Latrines Party of 20 men of R. Irish
turned up and carried the
journey at site of Tobruk [illegible];
all the latrines filled in.

At [illegible] to [illegible] to
be a few removed from the
position of the old latrines and
fixed temporarily in the afternoon
[illegible] with [illegible]. No [illegible] of
[illegible] with [illegible] from old
latrines and then the ground was
[illegible] up [illegible] with [illegible]

Refuse and Garbage removed daily
from all [illegible]
One cesspit emptied at [illegible]
[illegible] R.A.R.E.

Sanitary party of 2 N.C.Os & 13 men
sent to 5th [illegible] [illegible]

J. Clayton
[illegible] RAMC

112

complain that practically the
whole of the advanced part of
their area is dirty, and have
asked for a sanitary party
to supervise work.

In BÉTHUNE, sanitary work is now
proceeding as organised yesterday.

/ Clayton
Lieut RAMC

1 Case of measles disinfected
today at BEUVRY.
J. Clayton

A.D. of S. 2nd Divn.

Report of Sanitary Officer. July 1st 1915

BETHUNE. 5th Inf. Brigade vacated their billets in BETHUNE yesterday and left them all fairly clean; all latrine buckets emptied and outside yards clean, but some of the rooms inside might have been swept out better. No head complaint to make about any of their billets.

Visited BEUVEQUIN this morning; arranged to withdraw sanitary party on Saturday, by which time work should be completed except the work which can only be tackled by pump & cart cart.

Went to 5th Inf Brigade H.Q. on La Bassée Canal this afternoon on receipt of a wire. They

A.D.M.S. 2nd Div.
Report of Sanitary Officer. July 2.

Inspected most of the by billets in BETHUNE. Sanitary work now proceeding satisfactorily, but there are still accumulations of refuse scattered about in various parts of the Town and these require attention immediately.

Cesspits emptied today at Tobacco Factory and ORPHANAGE.

James Clayton
Lieut. R.A.M.C.

A.D.M.S. 2nd Div
Report of Sanitary Officer. July 2nd

BETHUNE. Sanitation work in the town continued as yesterday.
Refuse collected from No.6. F.A at ANNEZIN.

4 lorry loads refuse carted from ANNEZIN to Tobacco factory.

Removal of refuse and manure from HOTEL DE GARCONS is now complete.

Sanitary parties withdrawn today from ANNEZIN and from OBLINGHEM.

Arrangements made to send out a Sanitary party of 1 N.C.O and 10 men to 5th Inf. Brigade for organisation of work in area LE QUESNOY, LE PREOL and Headquarters 5th Inf. Bgd.

James Clayton
Lieut. R.A.M.C.

2ND DIVISION
MEDICAL

NO.11 SANITARY SECTION

JAN - DEC 1916

WAR DIARY

of

No.11. Sanitary Section- 2nd Division

for the Months of January and February & March, 1916.

War Diary

No 11 Sanitary Section

2nd Division

Place & Date.	Events.
BUSNES. Jan 1st. 1916.	Divided present "rest" area occupied by 2nd Div. into 4 parts for purposes of sanitary work.

i. **5th Brigade area.** H.Q. at COTTES. Sergt. ELLISON and 2 other N.C.Os of Sanitary Section attached for supervision of this area.

ii. **6th Bge. area.** H.Q. at HAM-en-ARTOIS. Sergt. TYLER and 2 other N.C.Os.

iii. **99th Bge. area.** H.Q. at GONNEHEM. Corp. HOWARTH and 2 other N.C.Os.

iv. **H.Q. of 2nd Div.** with area occupied by Div. Train and Div. H.Q. Troops. H.Q. at BUSNES. Corp. RIDDELL and CORP. CLARKE.

All the above despatched to work today.

Jan 2nd. Vidange pump & tank cart obtained from BETHUNE for cesspit at H.Q. Chateau.
Visited following billetting areas:—
2nd South Staffs at LE CORNET BOURDOIS
1st Kings at LA PIERRIÈRE.
17th Middlesex at BUSNES east.

Percentage Sickness for week ending
Jan 2nd = 0.81%.
(Weekly % Sickness is —

$$\frac{\text{Total Admissions of Sick per Week} \times 100}{\text{Average Strength of the Division}}$$

5th Scottish Rifles 32nd Div. —
40 men isolated at LA PIERRIERE
as diphtheria contacts.

Jan 3rd.   Visited billets of
            1st East Anglian R.E. at CORNET BOURDOIS
            and bathhouse at "   "
            1st Herts at HAM.

Jan 4th.   Visited 5th Brig. HQ. at COTTES
            and 2nd. Ox & Bucks at COTTES.
            Drains at 5th Brig HQ require repairs.

Jan 5th.   Visited billets of 22nd Royal Fusiliers
            at L'ECLÈME. 130 men of
            Machine Gun Section and Transport
            of this battalion are isolated
            owing to having gone into a billet
            vacated on the 27th December 1915
            by a case of Chicken Pox in the
            21st R.F of 32nd Div.

Jan 6th — Visited 13th Essex at HANQUEVILLE and 2nd Div Supply Column on BOSNES – LILLERS road.

Jan 7th — Visited 5th Brig. H.Q. at COTTES. Arranged drainage work & for emptying of cesspit.
Many Units asking for material for erection of proper covered latrines & for ablution places. Arranged a scheme with C.R.E.; pioneers of Units to commence the work; material to be drawn from 'RE' Store in BETHUNE.

Jan 8th — Two platoons 5th Scottish Rifles, diphtheria contacts at La Pierrière, sent back to duty with 33rd Div.
Chicken Pox case at L'ECLEME.
Disinfected all blankets of Machine Gun Section & Transport of 22nd R.F. in Foden Steam Disinfector. Both billets also disinfected with formalin. Visited L'ECLEME and 99th Brig. H.Q. at GONNEHEM.

Jan 9th.   Sick Percentage for the week 0.85%

Jan 10th.   3 p/H.I men attached as
            2nd
            bricklayers to this Section
            returned off leave on 9th inst
            were returned to their battalion
            today.
            Pte. PATTERSON 2nd H.I. attached
            to this Section as carpenter
            from 2nd Div. Company returned
            off leave 24 hours late. Was
            arrested + sent for trial by O.C.
            2nd Div Coy.
            Visited Gomiehem. C.S.M
            case at 100th Field Ambulance.
            Billet disinfected. Blankets
            steam sterilised on 12th inst.

Jan 11th.   Visited FOUQUEREUIL and
            BÉRGUETTE to provide latrine
            accommodation for whole of
            2nd Div in case of movement

Jan 12.   Entraining movement orders
            received.
            Visited Manqueville (13th Essex)
            and Busnes East (17th Middlesex)

Jan. 16.   No 2093 Lance Corporal (Acting Sergt.) ROBERTS, E, awarded D.C.M. for good work at Festubert, Vermelles, Windy Corner etc.

Jan 18.   Prepared for move into BETHUNE.

Jan 19.   9.0 am. moved Section to BETHUNE.

Jan 20.   Divisional Area organised as before into 3 Brigade areas and one H.Q. area with Sanitary parties attached to each.

February

Feb. 20 — 2nd Div. Sanitary Section removed to BUSNES for few days before Division leaves for new area.
Two Inf. Brigades in Reserve area BUSNES and GONNEHEM.
Sanitary parties attached to each

Feb. 27 — Returned Section to BETHUNE.

Feb. 29 — Whole Division moved to new area and took over French line CALONNE – BULLY GRENAY – AIX-NOULETTE sectors with Div. H.Q. at SAINS EN GOHELLE.

March

March 1st — Organised Sanitary work of Div. as follows –
i. H.Q. area at SAINS EN GOHELLE
ii. 6th Brigade area, CALONNE and BULLY GRENAY.
iii. 5th Brigade area part of BULLY GRENAY, FOSSE 10.
iv. 99th Brigade area AIX-NOULETTE to SOUCHEZ river, BOUVIGNY and BOYEFFLES.
Sanitary parties attached

to each of above. All three Inf. Brigades in the line. A fourth Inf Brigade from 23rd Div attached to 2nd Div. as Reserve & with H.Q. at HERSIN.
Sanitary work of the two towns HERSIN and BARLIN organised and put under Town Majors with P.B. men attached.

Shower Baths erected at BULLY GRENAY, AIX-NOULETTE and SAINS EN GOHELLE.

Complete Water Survey and Analyses of all waters in the Divisional area made from March 1st to March 12th.

All cases of infectious disease civilian & military investigated in Divisional area. Particular attention directed to cases of ENTERIC at Barlin and DIPHTHERIA and MEASLES at Fosse 10.

March 22nd. Section moved with Division to Reserve Area at BRUAY.

March 23rd — At BRUAY organised sanitary work of new Reserve Area — practically new to British Troops.
H.Q. 2nd Div. at BRUAY.
6th Inf. Bde. at BRUAY
5th Inf. Bde. at DIVION
99th " " at DIVION.
Area extended to COMBLAIN-CHATELAIN, CALONNE-RICOUART, OURTON, LA COMTE.
As practically no sanitary arrangements — latrines, incinerators, ablution places, &c — existed the whole of them had to be constructed in the course of the first 3 weeks.

March 29th — Complete scheme of sanitation for the Town of BRUAY prepared and all material drawn from R.E.
Commenced work on above scheme and by April 17th more than half completed.

Summary of Infectious Diseases
for first 3 months Jan, Feb, March
1916.

	Jan	Feb	March
ENTERIC	1	0	2
PARATYPHOID	0	2	1
DIPHTHERIA	2	2	2
SCARLET FEVER	0	2	2
MEASLES	1	0	8
GERMAN MEASLES	2	1	2
Cerebrospinal MENINGITIS	1	2	0

Above figures represent the
number of military cases in 2nd Div.

War Diary

No 11 Sanitary Section
2nd Division.

for April, May, ~~June, 1916~~

April

April 9th — Two N.C.Os. of Sanitary Section sent out and attached to Section of No.5. F.A. in 1st Army Training Area for the purpose of carrying out disinfection of cases of infectious disease occurring in the Inf. Brigade undergoing manoeuvres.

April 18th — Half of BRUAY sanitary scheme completed; remainder of material handed over to Sanitary Section 23rd Div.

April 19th — Moved from reserve area to front area. H.Q. again at SAINS EN GOUHELLE.

April 20th — Sanitary parties attached to Brigade H.Qs etc. in the Divisional area as shown below :—

6th Bde HQ at Bully Grenay
    2 NCOs 1 man
5th Bde HQ at Bully Grenay
    3 NCOs 1 man
99th Bde HQ at Aix Noulette
    3 NCOs 1 man

Town of BARLIN. — 1 NCO
　　　attached to Town Major
Town of HERSIN. — 1 NCO
　　　attached to Town Major.

April 20th
to May 12th

Sanitary work consisted chiefly of providing Units with material for construction of wooden covers for latrines of the deep pit (covered) fly-proof ~~summer~~ type. These were put in large ~~numbers~~ into trenches (6th & 5th Brigade fronts, but not in 99th Brigade front) and all over the area in billets.

Experiments carried out with "C" solution as a fly-killer and for destroying fly maggots in fresh stable manure. It was found to be an excellent fly killer and deodorant but as it will not mix readily with water, its practical use is very limited.

Other work consisted in the

organisation of local manure dumps throughout the whole area. As flies breed readily in fresh horse manure the proper disposal of all horse manure is a matter of extreme urgency where such large numbers of horses exist. Such large quantities of manure can not be easily burned on account of the enormous amount of labour required.

It was therefore decided to fix on local manure dumps to which all units in their vicinity should cart their manure, and that these manure heaps should then be treated twice weekly by covering with earth, burning over the surface, or spraying with cresol or C. Solution. Such dumps were established at

BARLIN (3 dumps)
HERSIN (2 dumps) and COUPIGNY,
BOUVIGNY
BOYEFFLES (2 dumps)
Fosse 10 (2 dumps)
Sains en Gohelle.

COUPIGNY HUT ENCAMPMENT.

From April 30th to May 11th at the above encampment a large 34 seat bucket covered latrine with urinal, and large destructor for burning camp refuse and faeces were built and completed.

Infectious Disease

Summary for April

ENTERIC GROUP	2 cases
GERMAN MEASLES	4 —
SCARLET FEVER	2 —
MEASLES	13 —

XI Sanitary Sec
WO 95 Tb

WAR DIARY
or
INTELLIGENCE SUMMARY.
(Erase heading not required.)

Army Form C. 2118.

Hour, Date, Place	Summary of Events and Information	Remarks and references to Appendices
May 13th	2nd Division moved out of the line into reserve area of IV th Corps. HQ. going to Chateau at La Comté. Sanitary Section with HQ. of La Comté.	
May 14th	On Brigade (99th) back with Division in Reserve Area. 5th Brigade at HERSIN; 6th Brigade still in the line at CAMONNE. Sent out 1 sanitary party to 99th Bde. at BRUAY to arrange sanitary work in that area, and 1 party to Divisional H.Q. at Chateau where latrines, incinerators, ablution places etc. have to be constructed.	
May 15th to 19th	Continued work as above. Efforts made to get timber from Div' R.E. for sanitary purposes e.g. construction of covered pit	

WAR DIARY
or
INTELLIGENCE SUMMARY.
(Erase heading not required.)

Army Form C. 2118.

Hour, Date, Place	Summary of Events and Information	Remarks and references to Appendices
May 19th	Latrines for the Div. area met with little success as usual. The difficulties experienced in this respect arise from (1) rapid moving about of units from place to place so that their pioneers can get no field work done (2) delay in getting materials from R.E. 5th Brigade moved back from HERSIN to DIVION area. Sanitary party of 6 3 N.CO and 1 man attached to this Brigade too.	
May 21st	Moved sanitary section from one part of the Corps to another part, under orders of Corps Commandant h.q. Div. No. 11160 Pte. GROVER brought up by Sgt. TYLER R of sanitary section for insubordination. Remanded	

WAR DIARY or INTELLIGENCE SUMMARY

Army Form C. 2118.

Hour, Date, Place	Summary of Events and Information	Remarks and references to Appendices
May 22nd	Div. HQ moved temporarily up in support of 47th Div. at VIMY Ridge. 99th and 6th Brigades moved up. 5th Brigade remained in DIVION area. Infantry.	
May 24th	Advance standing by to move. Called in all outstanding parties of Infantry Schools.	
May 25th	Under orders of ADAMS and Div. moved down and up to GROUCHIN-LEGER.	
May 26th	Moved Standing baton to CHATEAU de la HAIE where rejoined 2nd Div. HQ. One standing party of 3 N.C.O. and 1 man left with 5th Bde HQ at FRESNICOURT. Organised area into 4 parts.	
May 27th	H.Q. Area including Chateau de la HAIE, PETIT SERVINS, GRAND SERVINS and GOUY-SERVINS.	

WAR DIARY
or
INTELLIGENCE SUMMARY.
(Erase heading not required.)

Army Form C. 2118.

Hour, Date, Place	Summary of Events and Information	Remarks and references to Appendices
	2. 5th Bde (Reserve) area including FRESNICOURT, GAUCHIN-LEGAL, MAGNICOURT, FREVILLERS, ESTRÉE-CAUCHIE, CAUCOURT and part of GOUY-SERVINS.	
	3. Left Brigade in the Line (6th Bde) including VILLERS-AU-BOIS, CARENCY, ABLAIN-ST-NAZAIRE and two battalions in the line.	
	4. Right Brigade in the Line (99th Bde) including part of VILLERS-AU-BOIS, CAMBLAIN L'ABBÉ, CABARET ROUGE, and two battalions in the line.	
May 28th	Securing parties of 3 N.C.O. and 1 man sent out to each of 6th and 99th Brigade H.Qs.	
May 29th	Visited 6th & 99th Bde HQs, Town Major VILLERS-AU-BOIS, CARENCY, ABLAIN ST-NAZAIRE.	

Army Form C. 2118.

WAR DIARY
or
INTELLIGENCE SUMMARY.
(Erase heading not required.)

Instructions regarding War Diaries and Intelligence Summaries are contained in F.S. Regs., Part II. and the Staff Manual respectively. Title pages will be prepared in manuscript.

Hour, Date, Place	Summary of Events and Information	Remarks and references to Appendices
May 30th. 1916.	Visited VILLERS-au-BOIS re water supply. Memorandum on the subject sent in to ADMS. re forwarding to R.E. concerning water supplies in this area.	
May 31st. 1916.	Between May 28th and 31st. the whole area has been surveyed with a view to putting into practice a complete system of course fluid (Horrocks) latrines. Estimates of the amount of timber required for this purpose in each billet area have been sent in through the whole Arrangement to ADMS. for authority to Div. train from RE. to issue to Units.	

Summary of Infectious Diseases in 2nd Division for May.

MEASLES ——— 5 cases
GERMAN MEASLES ——— 5 ”
PARATYPHOID "A" ——— 1 case
DIPHTHERIA ——— 2 cases

2nd Division

No 11 Sanitary Section

Army Form C. 2118.

WAR DIARY
or
INTELLIGENCE SUMMARY.
(Erase heading not required.)

Instructions regarding War Diaries and Intelligence Summaries are contained in F.S. Regs., Part II. and the Staff Manual respectively. Title pages will be prepared in manuscript.

Hour, Date, Place	Summary of Events and Information	Remarks and references to Appendices
June 1st.	Divisional H.Q. shelled from 9.20 to 10.40 p.m. at CHATEAU de la HAIE.	
June 2nd.	Court Martial Case No 11110 Pte. GARNIER, E. 1st KING'S attached to No 11 Sanitary Section inder tried by F.G.C.M. 6th Inf. Brigade at VILLERS-AU-BOIS.	
June 3rd. CHATEAU L'ABBÉ	Divisional H.Q. moved from Chateau de la HAIE to CHATEAU L'ABBÉ. Sanitary Section moved into new billets at the latter place. O.C. Sanitary Section on leave to the end. Capt. G.D. SHERWOOD 5th Field Ambulance temporarily doing duty.	
June 3rd to 15th	The following Sanitary work organised in the 2nd Div area:— Ashermen—were obtained for trials for latrine covers (3 kinds system) as per estimate of May 31st. and drawn from R.E. and distributed to units. MANURE DUMPS established at the following places:—	

WAR DIARY
or
INTELLIGENCE SUMMARY.
(Erase heading not required.)

Army Form C. 2118.

Instructions regarding War Diaries and Intelligence Summaries are contained in F. S. Regs., Part II. and the Staff Manual respectively. Title pages will be prepared in manuscript.

Hour, Date, Place	Summary of Events and Information	Remarks and references to Appendices
CAMBRAIN L'ABBÉ	— 2 dumps to serve H.Q. Transport; 2nd Signal Coy; to Coy. water Train; and various small units in the place.	
VILLERS aux BOIS	— 1 dump. — Field Coys. R.E.	
MAISNIL BOUCHÉ	— 1 dump. R.E. H.Q. and Coy. R.E. in huts	
ESTRÉE-CAUCHIE	— 1 dump, to serve 1 batter. Transport and 1 Field Ambulance	
GAUCHIN-LEGAL	— 1 dump to serve all battery wagon lines.	
CAUCOURT	— 1 dump, to serve the D.A.C.	
GRAND SERVINS	— 1 dump, to serve 1 Inf. Brigade Transport	
PETIT SERVINS } GOUY SERVINS }	— 1 dump, to serve 1½ Brig. Transport & Field Coys. R.E.	

Sanitary work at ESTRÉE-CAUCHIE, CAMBRAIN L'ABBÉ

Army Form C. 2118.

WAR DIARY
or
INTELLIGENCE SUMMARY.
(Erase heading not required.)

Instructions regarding War Diaries and Intelligence Summaries are contained in F.S. Regs., Part II. and the Staff Manual respectively. Title pages will be prepared in manuscript.

Hour, Date, Place	Summary of Events and Information	Remarks and references to Appendices
June 14th	GRAND, PETIT and GOUY-SERVINS, and VILLERS-au-BOIS has been organised under the respective 3 Town Majors who are authorised to carry out all measures necessary for general cleanness of the places, street cleaning, cleaning billets, disinfection of houses & manure pits - by obtaining fatigue parties from the different units in these places. The work is organised by & Sanitary Section and supervised by his N.C.O's. return troops attached to Division :- 2½ Battalions of ROYAL NAVAL DIVISION. 2 Field Coys R.E. of " 2 entire batteries " 2 Pioneer Battalions, changing from time to time - 13th Yorkon, 14th Worcester, 10th D.C.L.I. 2nd R.M. L.I.	

Army Form C. 2118.

WAR DIARY
or
INTELLIGENCE SUMMARY.
(Erase heading not required.)

Instructions regarding War Diaries and Intelligence Summaries are contained in F.S. Regs., Part II. and the Staff Manual respectively. Title pages will be prepared in manuscript.

Hour, Date, Place	Summary of Events and Information	Remarks and references to Appendices
June 15th	As all these extra troops are sanitary arrangements have to be made & sanitary latrine required from leave.	
June 16th	1st & 2nd tanks asked for for the new battalions R.N.D. 1 Case of Dysentery occurred in 2nd Field Coy R.N.D. which had previously been in Gallipoli. Measures of necessity for tests for making more far reaching for these which are improved on the Division.	
June 18th	Two N. Cos of Sanitary Section went to Helles at FORV-SERVES to see to their better supervision of the camps. The amount of transport at our then services is manure protection is difficult and requires in getting horses, earth &labour for carting manure to dumps and for subsequently burying it there.	

(73989) W4141—463. 400,000. 9/14. H.&J.Ltd. Forms/C. 2118/10.

Army Form C. 2118.

WAR DIARY
or
INTELLIGENCE SUMMARY.
(Erase heading not required.)

Instructions regarding War Diaries and Intelligence Summaries are contained in F.S. Regs., Part II. and the Staff Manual respectively. Title pages will be prepared in manuscript.

Hour, Date, Place	Summary of Events and Information	Remarks and references to Appendices
June 19th	Visited all recent work in the area in the question & noted any taken up largely by Tramway Coy. O.C. Units. More supervision on part of Divisions. Seton necessary. Overcame difficulties of ① labour ② horses & carts at each place in turn. ③ Paper implements. Organized light tramstation in middle of the R.W.D. and also in the front part of the line, in support trenches and in communication trenches. The amount of trucks obtained from R.E. for making proper covers for latrines has been a great improvement on last month otherwise. The by the Platoons — the bed for humans — is now very general throughout the whole area.	
June 20 to 6. 29th		

(73989) W4141—463. 400,000. 9/14. H.&J.Ltd. Forms/C. 2118/10.

Army Form C. 2118.

WAR DIARY
or
INTELLIGENCE SUMMARY.
(Erase heading not required.)

Instructions regarding War Diaries and Intelligence Summaries are contained in F.S. Regs., Part II. and the Staff Manual respectively. Title pages will be prepared in manuscript.

Hour, Date, Place	Summary of Events and Information	Remarks and references to Appendices
June 30th	General improvement also shown recently in the higher health of men. Raindrops in much better state. They are now squared up regularly and covered with earth and the street edges of the camp Mosquitoes unusually cleared of "C" pollution. Flies exceedingly few in the whole area for this time of year. Summary of Infectious Diseases /Nature/ DIPHTHERIA — 1 case ~~Measles~~ MEASLES — 2 cases DYSENTERY — 1 case from Royal Naval Division NO ENTERIC. Taylor Capt O.C. Sanitary Section	

2.

War Diary of No. 11 Sanitary Section, 2nd Division
for July 1916.

Vol 22

W Taylor
Capt.
O. Sanitary Sec.
2nd Div.

2.8.16.

COMMITTEE FOR THE
MEDICAL HISTORY OF THE WAR
Date 13 SEP. 1916

WAR DIARY
or
INTELLIGENCE SUMMARY.
(Erase heading not required.)

Army Form C. 2118.

Hour, Date, Place	Summary of Events and Information	Remarks and references to Appendices
July 1st to 12th	General situation work throughout the area continues. Maison Blanche kept in good order by continual labour. Constructional work. — Commun[ication] pit between new "general transport" shale area.	
July 13th	Movements of trucks moved for alteration between ESTREE CAUCHIE and CAMBLAIN L'ABBE are made. Winter Brigade H.Q. and trenches at CABARET ROUGE and ZOUAVE VALLEY.	
July 15th	Water a spring in ZOUAVE VALLEY with a carpenter to see about alterations, improvements in the water supply here. Reservoir not ready. Has of them spring which is good water.	

WAR DIARY
or
INTELLIGENCE SUMMARY.
(Erase heading not required.)

Army Form C. 2118.

Instructions regarding War Diaries and Intelligence
Summaries are contained in F.S. Regs., Part II.
and the Staff Manual respectively. Title pages
will be prepared in manuscript.

Hour, Date, Place	Summary of Events and Information	Remarks and references to Appendices
July 16th	IVth Corps Rt. (Motor Supplies) slowly improving well in CARRIAGE N L'ABBE. Order to move to LA COMTE.	
July 17th	Sergt. PEER of this Section sent to hospital to convalesce. Recalled all motor parties to H.Q.	
July 18th	Returned Pte. GARNER to his Unit (1st-King's) arriving 1.15 pm. Moved to LA COMTE.	
July 19th	L/Corp. FOSTER sent to hospital evacuated. Orders received to entrain at BRUAY on the 20th inst. at 3.30 pm.	
July 20th	Entrained at BRUAY 3.30 pm. Lorry proceeded by road to 6.29 pm. Arrived HQ at CORBIE when it arrived at 11.30 pm. Section detrained 1.50 am	

Army Form C. 2118.

WAR DIARY
or
INTELLIGENCE SUMMARY.
(Erase heading not required.)

Instructions regarding War Diaries and Intelligence Summaries are contained in F.S. Regs., Part II. and the Staff Manual respectively. Title pages will be prepared in manuscript.

Hour, Date, Place	Summary of Events and Information	Remarks and references to Appendices
July 21st.	On July 21st at LONGUEAU entrained AMIENS, and marched to billets at CORBIE, arriving 6.30 am.	
July 22nd.	Saturday taken with Officer in billets at CORBIE. Supervised Sunday arrangement of Divisional HQrs. Long Cont. B.A.R. to R.E. details for removal of Staff from LONGUEAU to CORBIE Station. "Q" Office arrangements for took tomorrow.	
July 23rd.	Long party to LONGUEAU station at 5 am. Proceeded to A.D.M.S. carrying everything direct. Others to my personnel from "Q" Office.	
July 24th.	Under orders from A.D.M.S. and Div. moved whole Sunday station at 7.30 am from CORBIE to billets at MÉAULTE.	
July 25th.	Moved Sanitary Section at 1.30 pm to CITADEL	

Army Form C. 2118.

WAR DIARY
or
INTELLIGENCE SUMMARY.
(Erase heading not required.)

Instructions regarding War Diaries and Intelligence Summaries are contained in F. S. Regs., Part II. and the Staff Manual respectively. Title pages will be prepared in manuscript.

Hour, Date, Place	Summary of Events and Information	Remarks and references to Appendices
July 25th	CORNER 2000 yards south of FRICOURT on the FRICOURT — BRAY road. Put Sanitary Section into tents here.	
July 26th	Organised sanitary arrangements for the new town. Water filters replenished at CITADEL.	
July 27th	H.Q. camp from FRICOURT. Took over from No. 5 Field Ambulance the men of sanitary section details to mount. Constructing a dug-out for No. 5 Field Ambulance Advanced Dressing Station at CARNOY.	
July 28th	Details 18 N.C.Os and men of Sanitary Section to proceed at 7.30 a.m. to report to O.C. No 5 Field Ambulance Dressing Station at north end of BERNAFAY WOOD. Here they were employed as stretcher bearers, evacuating wounded from the LONGUEVAL & BERNAFAY WOOD area	

WAR DIARY
or
INTELLIGENCE SUMMARY.
(Erase heading not required.)

Army Form C. 2118.

Hour, Date, Place	Summary of Events and Information	Remarks and references to Appendices
July 28th.	6.0 p.m. Relieved at 6.0 p.m. Owing to heavy shelling of all huts especially LONGUEVAL 5 casualties occurred amongst them all by shell fire about 4.30 p.m. on the main road at south end of LONGUEVAL. The following casualties occurred in the Sanitary Section acting in advanced trenches:— No. 2326 Pte. (Acty L/Cpl.) TAYLOR, J.H. — killed. No. 1637 Pte. HARRIS, A.R. — killed. No. 2091 Pte. (Acty Cpl) CLARKE, C. — wounded. No. 633 Pte. (Acty L/Cpl) COLLINS, F.W. — wounded. No. 39668 Pte. (Acty Cpl). PETERS, L.M. — shell shock. [Attached from No. 6. Field Ambulance]	
July 29th.	Arranged complete system of Narrow Gauge tramways to H.Q. Camp then — All water fetched from FRICOURT where there is	

WAR DIARY
or
INTELLIGENCE SUMMARY.
(Erase heading not required.)

Army Form C. 2118.

Instructions regarding War Diaries and Intelligence Summaries are contained in F.S. Regs., Part II. and the Staff Manual respectively. Title pages will be prepared in manuscript.

Hour, Date, Place	Summary of Events and Information	Remarks and references to Appendices
July 29th	a good steam pump supply. Sanitary Section with improvised tanks cart which does 4 journeys fetches 400 gallons which is stored in a tank and used for washing trenches purposes. 2nd Div. HQ two water carts, fetch 600 gallons which is partly stored in a barrel near HQ transport. R.A. HQ water cart fetches 200 gallons 2nd Div Signal water cart fetches 400 gallons which is partly stored in a barrel. Sanitary organised Staff carried on between Bray town + Longing relief Fatigue taken from Div.Cyclists Took up a Park of 24 relief stretchers taken on water tank to S.W. of MONTAUBAN and thence by foot to be taken half at N.W. end of BERNAFAY wood. Heavy shelling all day.	
July 30th		
July 31st		

Clayton Capt.
O.C. Sanitary Section 2nd Div

2nd Pas

No. 11 Sanitary Section

COMMITTEE FOR THE MEDICAL HISTORY OF THE WAR
Date 26 OCT 1916

War Diary of
   No 11 Sanitary Section
                    2nd Div.
   for August. 1916

WAR DIARY ~~Xl~~ Sanitary Army Form C. 2118.
or
INTELLIGENCE SUMMARY. 2 D M
(Erase heading not required.)

Instructions regarding War Diaries and Intelligence
Summaries are contained in F.S. Regs., Part II.
and the Staff Manual respectively. Title pages
will be prepared in manuscript.

Hour, Date, Place	Summary of Events and Information	Remarks and references to Appendices
August 1st.	Took up a party of F.A. Co trench at fire of MONTAUBAN. Thence carried implements and disinfectants up to west side of BERNAFAY wood and dealt with 4 behind dead horses — very bad. Heavy shelling all day.	Vol 2 3
August 2nd.	Collected large amount of disinfectants — 3 tons quicklime, and 3 tons of creol & chloride of lime to improve a disinfectant dump near the advanced Divisional Baths dump at S.W. end of BERNAFAY wood by cross roads — from Sqn S 28 d.2.2. Only tons of gothy stuff up worth ambulance can bring up with to carment horses put in lime and put gas up now to simply complete destruction of roads in parts high shell fire.	

Army Form C. 2118.

WAR DIARY
or
INTELLIGENCE SUMMARY.
(*Erase heading not required.*)

Instructions regarding War Diaries and Intelligence Summaries are contained in F. S. Regs., Part II. and the Staff Manual respectively. Title pages will be prepared in manuscript.

Hour, Date, Place	Summary of Events and Information	Remarks and references to Appendices
Aug 4th	Established disinfectant dump at the point mentioned and took up one carload. O.C. ambulance car at West PÉRONNE and post arranged to hand up the ammunition by empty cars going up. Heavy hostile barrage fire at various points on the roads all day. Sent up another lot of disinfectants to BERNAFAY wood. 1 N.C.O. and 1 man of sanitary section sent to WEST PÉRONNE and post for water duties — filling water cart at CARNOY and trucking up water in petrol tins by ambulance car to the BERNAFAY wood and DUBLIN trench and posts.	
Aug 5th – 7th	Attention given to sanitary duties at two A.D.S. camps –	

WAR DIARY
or
INTELLIGENCE SUMMARY.
(Erase heading not required.)

Army Form C. 2118.

Instructions regarding War Diaries and Intelligence Summaries are contained in F.S. Regs., Part II. and the Staff Manual respectively. Title pages will be prepared in manuscript.

Hour, Date, Place	Summary of Events and Information	Remarks and references to Appendices
Aug. 8th	at the CITADEL and MINDEN POST — and to 99th Inf. Brigade Camp. Any N.C.Os. men of Sanitary Section sent to Advanced Dressing Station CARNOY to help in directing and loading into horse ambulances of the walking wounded coming down from BERNAFAY wood.	
Aug. 11th	Withdrew 2 men on ration duties from West Personal Aid Post. Prepared to move Sanitary Section on 12th. Horse Transport that is am annexe will aid Div. Train. Two reinforcements arrived from Rouen Base Camp.	
Aug. 12th	Moved Sanitary Section at 2 p.m. to Kilos at TREUX.	
Aug. 13th	Three Reinforcements received. Orders receipt to entrain at MÉRICOURT L'ABBÉ at 5 p.m. to GOSIEUX detraining station & then proceed to PICQUIGNY. Lorry sent by road.	

Army Form C. 2118.

WAR DIARY
or
INTELLIGENCE SUMMARY.
(Erase heading not required.)

Instructions regarding War Diaries and Intelligence Summaries are contained in F. S. Regs., Part II. and the Staff Manual respectively. Title pages will be prepared in manuscript.

Hour, Date, Place	Summary of Events and Information	Remarks and references to Appendices
Aug. 14th	Sunday Service obtained at SALEUX and arrived at PICQUIGNY at 10 p.m.	
	Organise training arrangements in PICQUIGNY for front of 2nd Bn. H.R. and for 5th H.Gds. Bde. (huts); also for H.Q. and Bn. at BELLOY.	
Aug. 16th	Moved Sunday Service to VIGNACOURT by route march, arriving 6.30 p.m.	
Aug. 17th	Moved from VIGNACOURT by road to BERNAVILLE (about 9 miles), commenced start at 2 p.m., arrived at 5 p.m.	
Aug. 18th	Moved by road from BERNAVILLE to BUS-LES-ARTOIS, distance about 19 miles, arriving destination 5 p.m.	
Aug. 19th & 20th	At BUS-LES-ARTOIS. Went round new area with O.C. Facing Father Guards Division from whom	

(73989) W4141-463. 400,000. 9/14. H.&J.Ltd. Forms/C. 2118/10.

WAR DIARY
or
INTELLIGENCE SUMMARY.
(Erase heading not required.)

Army Form C. 2118.

Hour, Date, Place	Summary of Events and Information	Remarks and references to Appendices
Aug. 21st	We are taking over. Marched to COUVIN — distance 2½ miles. Put up tents/shelters in a hut and tents.	
Aug. 22nd	Commenced organisation of new area. Area divided into 4 parts — 3 Brigade areas and one H.Q. and tent area. Each Brigade is to throw into the line Attached Artillery [unclear] horses a train also (huts & horses) to each of the 4 areas. Commenced organisation of reserve dumps for whole area; arranged for fresh horses in various stables at various places. Schemes of instruction received from Reserve Army and from 5th Corps include provision of fly-proof tent & deep pit latrines in trenches, but if fly proof bucket type will necessitate, in all other huts which provide. This involves	

WAR DIARY or INTELLIGENCE SUMMARY.

Army Form C. 2118.

Hour, Date, Place	Summary of Events and Information	Remarks and references to Appendices
Aug 24th	A large amount of new organisation - reissue of maps, ammunition, extra bullets, concentration etc. Four hospital destructors asked for; other destruction of improved pattern to be built. Workshop lorries. Re-equipment. Photograph taken with plumbers, engineers & carpenters' tools was therefore found necessary. Indent to found submitted to Ordnance. Took on construction of new hangars commenced by German Division at AUTHIE. Lorries unlent permitted to "Q" branch for material, labour & tools to complete hangars. (6th Brigade - Inspected COUPELLES area. Capt. ROBERTS).	
Aug 25th		

Army Form C. 2118.

WAR DIARY
or
INTELLIGENCE SUMMARY.
(Erase heading not required.)

Instructions regarding War Diaries and Intelligence Summaries are contained in F.S. Regs., Part II. and the Staff Manual respectively. Title pages will be prepared in manuscript.

Hour, Date, Place	Summary of Events and Information	Remarks and references to Appendices
Aug. 29th	Visited 5th Bde. Trenches with Divisions.	
Aug. 30th	Conferences men with Div Brs. Promotion of Freemen NCO brought to the Establishment approved by O/C Reserve Station at A.P.O. This Bade., and made effective nominal Rs. No. 976 dated 10/7/15 to date from 18th Feb 1916:- No. 1663 Corporal G. ELLISON to be Acting Sergt. with pay. No. 2093 L/Cpl. E. ROBERTS - Acting Cpl. " " No. 2106. Pte. L McGOWAN - two guns to be Acting Lance Cpl. with pay.	
Aug. 31st	Inspected part of HQ area at COUIN with Divisions.	

Wayton Capt.
OC. No 11 Sanitary Section
2nd Div.

(73989) W4141—463. 400,000. 9/14. H.&J.Ltd. Forms/C. 2118/10.

140/1788

2nd Div

11th Sanitary Section

Sept 16

COMMITTEE FOR THE
MEDICAL HISTORY OF THE WAR
Date -2 DEC. 1916

War Diary of No 11 Sanitary Section 2nd Div. for month of September 1916.

Ulyton
Capt.

WAR DIARY or INTELLIGENCE SUMMARY

Army Form C. 2118.
N° 11 SANITARY SECTION — 2ND Div.

Hour, Date, Place	Summary of Events and Information	Remarks and references to Appendices
September 1st	Diagnosis of 7 cases of ENTERIC GROUP received from C.C.S. None all remained in 2nd Oxf. & Bucks L.I. (all "A" Company except one man in "B" Coy.) and all were sick from BUS-LES-ARTOIS on 22nd August. Sand made for cover. Laundry at AUTHIE handed over to 6 Div' R.E. for completion of construction.	Vol 24
Sept. 2nd	Went over 99th Brigade trenches (22nd & 23rd R.F. in the line). Latrines not getting in rapidly enough with Trench latrines — very important at present time owing to prevalence of dysentery & diarrhoea. Latrine covers requested from 2nd Oxf & Bucks L.I.	
" 3rd	Went round H.Q.'s town district. Completed scheme of MANURE DUMPS for the whole Div' area; forwarded to A.D.M.S. for publication.	

WAR DIARY
or
INTELLIGENCE SUMMARY.

(Erase heading not required.)

Army Form C. 2118.

Instructions regarding War Diaries and Intelligence Summaries are contained in F.S. Regs., Part II. and the Staff Manual respectively. Title pages will be prepared in manuscript.

Hour, Date, Place	Summary of Events and Information	Remarks and references to Appendices
Sept. 4th to 11th	On Routine Orders.	
Sept. 12th	Further improvement of Village Sanitation at COURCELLES, ARRAY-en-BOIS, COIGNEUX, COUIN and tr. legs. Large frames many incinerators built in each of first 3 places. Commenced extensions to Scully Dell Bathhouse with a view to purifying the body effluent by treatment with chloride of lime in a precipitation tank. R.E. did the work which turned out very possibly successful.	
Sept 13th	Commenced similar work at COUIN Bath house.	
Sept 14th	Took Lorry Disinfector of personnel round to put in charge of Sanitary Section. Proposed to get it in working order & work for company out at COIGNEUX in charge of Sanitary Section	Took Lorry Disinfector under mine arrangement as shown in Appendix I.
Sept. 15th	Up to present completed construction of 34 Lorry incinerators two at COUIN, one each at COIGNEUX & COURCELLES.	

(73989) W4141—463. 400,000. 9/14. H.&J.Ltd. Forms/C. 2118/10.

WAR DIARY
or
INTELLIGENCE SUMMARY.
(Erase heading not required.)

Army Form C. 2118.

Hour, Date, Place	Summary of Events and Information	Remarks and references to Appendices
Sept. 19th & 20th	Three Infantry Brigades came out of the line & moved to rest in Reserve Area – SARTON, VAUCHELLES and AUTHIE. Removed two of Smith patches in the framework, but leaving 1 N.C.O & man at SAILLY and 2 men at Bn. Headquarters. In the present there has been great improvement throughout the whole area in making latrines, fly proof; two trophies and 16th D.C.L.I. and one who two old artillery huts.	
Sept 21st	Commenced collection of material for building winter quarters for travelling kitchens in Cav IN-	
Sept 23rd	Commenced structure in attention of bonding; construction of office as for the above.	
Sept 25th	Took D.A.D.V.S. (Brigadier) Reserve Army round Inst of area. He found himself in very pleased with Sanitary improvements effected generally with system	

WAR DIARY
or
INTELLIGENCE SUMMARY.
(Erase heading not required.)

Army Form C. 2118.

Instructions regarding War Diaries and Intelligence Summaries are contained in F.S. Regs., Part II. and the Staff Manual respectively. Title pages will be prepared in manuscript.

Hour, Date, Place	Summary of Events and Information	Remarks and references to Appendices
Sept 26.	Ammunition dump & with the Village Instructors, but unable to see proper situation places constructed and arrangements of dumps with temporary note forwarded to Battalions. Majority of well & water storage tanks in the area have now been marked with white bands, those in the Tyne Frontier q.v. were kept for use in washing water only in Drinking water. Reservoir – Sap of Beaulin Powder – Intendina Cut. Received notification from Div. HQ to be standby to move at two hours notice. Gilleren matters from [Arrival] and cancelled.	

(73989) W4141—463. 400,000. 9/14. H.&J.Ltd. Forms/C. 2118/10.

Army Form C. 2118.

WAR DIARY
or
INTELLIGENCE SUMMARY.
(Erase heading not required.)

Instructions regarding War Diaries and Intelligence Summaries are contained in F. S. Regs., Part II. and the Staff Manual respectively. Title pages will be prepared in manuscript.

Hour, Date, Place	Summary of Events and Information	Remarks and references to Appendices
Sept. 26 to 29th	Carried on construction (Reorganisation in CO.I.N.) and inspection of Units in CO.I.N., COEUVRES & Mt. Loges. Commenced construction of a new Rest Home at BARTON.	
Sept. 30th	Summary of Infectious Diseases in 1st Div. for September: ENTERIC — 2 cases (1 civilian) PARATYPHOID — 1 case DYSENTERY — 3 ditto MUMPS — 1 ditto GERMAN MEASLES — 1 case TUBERCULOSIS (Lung) — 1 case TETANUS — 1 case (brought forward at from festering)	Capt. OC Sanitary Section 1st Div

2nd Division Q.3695/27.

STANDING ORDERS FOR THE FODEN THRESH DISINFECTOR.

1. The Foden Thresh Disinfector and its personnel now form part of the Divisional Sanitary Section and all applications for its use will be addressed to the O.C. of that Unit.

2. Normally, it will be allotted to each Infantry Brigade in turn for two consecutive days a week and it will be at the disposal of Divisional Headquarters one day a week. The programme will be as follows:-

Sunday	-	Divisional Headquarters.
Monday	-	5th Inf. Brigade.
Tuesday	-	"
Wednesday	-	6th Inf. Brigade.
Thursday	-	"
Friday	-	99th Inf. Brigade.
Saturday	-	"

    Alterations which it may be desirable to introduce during any one week will be arranged between the O.C. Divisional Sanitary Section and the Brigade concerned.

3. R.A. and R.E. will apply to Infantry Brigades, in whose area they are, for the use of the Disinfector on Infantry Brigade days. Other Divisional Troops will apply to the O.C. Divisional Sanitary Section for its use on the Divisional Headquarters day. Applications should reach the above officer by noon the day previous and the number of hours for which needed will be stated.

4. Orders for the move of the disinfector should be conveyed through the Brigade in whose area it is working. Brigades should assist one another by ensuring that the disinfector leaves their area for its next destination either the same day when finished with, or very early the next morning.

5. The actual working of the disinfector is under the direction of the N.C.O., R.A.M.C. in charge. He will keep a daily log of articles treated (recording Units concerned) and will render it weekly to the O.C. Divisional Sanitary Section.

6. The personnel of the disinfector will be rationed and billetted by the Brigade in whose area it is working. When not with Brigades they will draw rations from the Divisional Sanitary Section. Care is to be taken that the men receive the same rations as are being issued to other troops. This has not always been done.

7. The Senior Supply Officer will arrange for the supply of suitable steam coal. This will be delivered to the Sanitary Section or in Brigade areas as required.

8. Units employing the disinfector will provide all fatigue parties necessary and arrange for water.

9. The disinfector can deal with 80 blankets, or their equivalent, per hour.

10. It will be out of work for two days per month for cleaning.

11. These instructions cancel those issued under 2/Divnl. No. Q.3695/16 dated 5th April, 1916.

Lieut. Colonel.
A.A. & Q.M.G. 2nd Division.

22/9/16.

140/1788

2nd Division

11th Sanitary Section

Oct 1916

COMMITTEE FOR THE
MEDICAL HISTORY OF THE WAR
Date -2 DEC. 1916

War Diary of
No. 11 Sanitary Section
2nd Division, for
October 1916

J Clayton
Capt.

WAR DIARY
or
INTELLIGENCE SUMMARY.

(Erase heading not required.)

Army Form C. 2118.

XI Corps Auxiliary

Hour, Date, Place	Summary of Events and Information	Remarks and references to Appendices
Oct. 1st.	Prepared to move whole of transport and stores on 3rd inst.	See file 2/5
Oct. 2nd.	Visited new H.Q. Camp at BERTRANCOURT with Base rep. with a view to getting up proper bivouac arrangements between working parties, watercarts etc as practically nothing had been constructed.	
Oct. 3rd.	8. am. moved Cavalry section to X Camp at BERTRANCOURT. Commenced construction of bivouacs etc for HQ camp and extension of new bivouacs at work camp. About 24 carpenters and labourers at work in these. 20 labourers in attendance and work completed.	
Oct. 4th — 6th	4 Officers returns, 1 NCOs returns, & returns between 2 reinforcements, & working parties with bombing pits.	

Army Form C. 2118.

WAR DIARY
or
INTELLIGENCE SUMMARY.
(Erase heading not required.)

Instructions regarding War Diaries and Intelligence Summaries are contained in F. S. Regs., Part II. and the Staff Manual respectively. Title pages will be prepared in manuscript.

Hour, Date, Place	Summary of Events and Information	Remarks and references to Appendices
Oct 7th	Moved to H.Q. camp at HEDAUVILLE. Camp very dirty & latrine accommodation not sufficient for either Officers or men, to commence construction improvement work again.	
Oct 8th – 10th	Carried on above work with all carpenters, plumbers & labour available.	
Oct. 11th	Completed new arrangement with the three Infantry Brigades whereby 3 NCOs and 1 man of the sanitary section should be attached permanently to Inf. Brigade H.Q.s and these men will work under the O.C. sanitary section to carry out the supervision & improvement of the sanitation of all units in the Brigade area. The parties are under the O.C.	

Army Form C. 2118.

WAR DIARY
or
INTELLIGENCE SUMMARY.
(Erase heading not required.)

Instructions regarding War Diaries and Intelligence Summaries are contained in F.S. Regs., Part II. and the Staff Manual respectively. Title pages will be prepared in manuscript.

Hour, Date, Place	Summary of Events and Information	Remarks and references to Appendices
	Train left for aerodrome, & we merely billeted & returned homewards with Lt. Bryan MP.	
	9 am Oct 11th - test out there three pilots in charge of	
	Capt. Bilum (5th Brigade)	
	" Roberts (1st ")	
	" Turnbulow (4th ")	
Oct 12th to 17th	Evacuation of the villages of PICQUIGNY, LEALVILLERS, RAINCHEVAL, ARQUEVES and HÉDAUVILLE under the supervision Town Majors was attended to. Large concentration of troops in all these villages necessitated extra sanitary arrangements.	
Oct 18th	Orders received to move to BERTRANCOURT with Div. Headquarters. Moved further down to X camp BERTRANCOURT by 3 pm.	

Army Form C. 2118.

WAR DIARY
or
INTELLIGENCE SUMMARY.
(Erase heading not required.)

Instructions regarding War Diaries and Intelligence Summaries are contained in F.S. Regs., Part II. and the Staff Manual respectively. Title pages will be prepared in manuscript.

Hour, Date, Place	Summary of Events and Information	Remarks and references to Appendices
Oct. 19.	Took on organisation & construction of H.Q. Camp & F.X. Camp BERTEAUCOURT.	
Oct. 20.	Attached 1 N.C.O. (Cpl. Chappell) to Camp Commandant of MAILLY WOOD for tactical supervision of the Camp from in the event.	
Oct. 21.	Laid out a fatigue party from 6th Brigade to put up latrines at the new advanced Rouldens at BEAUFORT.	
Oct. 24th.	Received orders from 2 Army's in the event of active operations on this front to detail 1 N.C.O. & man in readiness to select & recommend from BEAUFORT Army station for evacuation & new of arriving Motor ambulance numbered from the Somme and the Collecting Post in	

WAR DIARY
or
INTELLIGENCE SUMMARY.
(*Erase heading not required.*)

Army Form C. 2118.

Instructions regarding War Diaries and Intelligence Summaries are contained in F.S. Regs., Part II. and the Staff Manual respectively. Title pages will be prepared in manuscript.

Hour, Date, Place	Summary of Events and Information	Remarks and references to Appendices
Oct. 25th.	5th Avenue to the "Red House" Dressing Station at Mailly-Maillet. Sent up N.C.O. in charge of these two parties to reconnoitre the routes of evacuation. Improvements, and withdrew altogether 8 men from & this Poignon & these further parties and HQ party for the above purpose.	
Oct. 26th.	Battle at BERTRANCOURT opened.	
Oct. 27th to 31st	Commencement of active operations continually And HQ from day to day, to carry on Tunnel Shafts Improvements in BERTRANCOURT, BEAUSSART and Beaumont-Richeux, and in MAILLY.	

No. 736 Staff-Serj. Hutchinson of this Section received Meritorious Service Medal

Army Form C. 2118.

WAR DIARY
or
INTELLIGENCE SUMMARY.
(Erase heading not required.)

Instructions regarding War Diaries and Intelligence Summaries are contained in F.S. Regs., Part II. and the Staff Manual respectively. Title pages will be prepared in manuscript.

Hour, Date, Place	Summary of Events and Information	Remarks and references to Appendices
	Summary of Infectious Diseases notified during October 1916.	
	Enteric. 11 cases	
	Paratyphoid "A" 4 "	
	" "B" 11 "	
	Dysentery 10 "	
	Diphtheria 2 "	
	Scarlet Fever 1 "	
	Measles 1 "	
	German Measles 0	
	C.S.M. 0	
		Wrayton Capt. D.A.D.M.S. 31.11.16

140/346

No 11 Sanitary Section

COMMITTEE FOR THE
MEDICAL HISTORY OF THE WAR
Date -3 JAN.1917

WAR DIARY / INTELLIGENCE SUMMARY

Army Form C. 2118.

11 Sanctuary Wood 26

Hour, Date, Place	Summary of Events and Information	Remarks and references to Appendices
November 1st to 12th.	Sanitation of the following places received attention:— Acheux Wood (huts), Bertrancourt, Beauvart and Beauvart Redhead, Mailly and Mailly Wood (huts). Orders received for commencement of further operations against the enemy on our Div front.	
November 12th	Ammunition personnel moved by ADMS to stations of stretcher bearer personnel (see October 24th) carried out. Took up NCOs + men to the "Red Horn", Mailly, and distributed them, 4 to the Avenue and 4 to the 5th Avenue for collection and direction of walking wounded.	
Nov. 13th	Battle commenced 5.45 am. Many prisoners taken and parties of them were drawn for carrying in wounded on stretchers.	

Army Form C. 2118.

WAR DIARY
or
INTELLIGENCE SUMMARY.
(Erase heading not required.)

Hour, Date, Place	Summary of Events and Information	Remarks and references to Appendices
Nov. 14th.	Obtained 17 German prisoners from APPL's coy and were three to bury 3 dead horses lying by the side of the windmill between the Redoubt and the Somme.	
Nov. 15th	Visited our posts at the Somme.	
Nov. 16th	Withdrew half of the posts from the Somme. Visited posts in St Avenue.	
Nov. 17th	Withdrew the posts from Somme & St Avenue.	
Nov. 19th	Moved from BERTRANCOURT to MARIEUX.	
Nov. 21st	Moved from MARIEUX to DOULLENS.	
Nov. 23rd	Moved from DOULLENS to BERNAVILLE.	
Nov. 27th	Moved from BERNAVILLE to YVRENCH. Moved from YVRENCH to BRAILLY.	

Army Form C. 2118.

WAR DIARY
or
INTELLIGENCE SUMMARY.
(Erase heading not required.)

Instructions regarding War Diaries and Intelligence Summaries are contained in F. S. Regs., Part II. and the Staff Manual respectively. Title pages will be prepared in manuscript.

Hour, Date, Place	Summary of Events and Information	Remarks and references to Appendices
Nov. 25th 6.30 a.m.	Commenced operations of hostility took in the Divisional area. As the men is is practically now one vast fast [area] of occupation by British troops the existing sanitary arrangements are absolutely nil. — no latrines, incinerators, baths, washing places, drying rooms, laundry etc. Arrangements [?] to provide for construction work. Also the whole area traversed for quantities of material required, — position of divisional latrines, drying rooms etc. —	

Army Form C. 2118.

WAR DIARY
or
INTELLIGENCE SUMMARY.

(Erase heading not required.)

Instructions regarding War Diaries and Intelligence Summaries are contained in F.S. Regs., Part II. and the Staff Manual respectively. Title pages will be prepared in manuscript.

Hour, Date, Place	Summary of Events and Information	Remarks and references to Appendices
	Summary of infectious diseases for the month.	
	Typhoid — 2 cases	
	Paratyphoid B — 1 case	
	Scarlet Fever — 1 case	
	Measles — 1 case	
	German Measles — 3 cases	
	Lobar Pneumonia — 2 cases	
	Dysentery — 6 cases	
	30.11.16.	Wright Capt. O. Sanitary Section ???

(73989) W4141—463. 400,000. 9/14. H.&J.Ltd. Forms/C. 2118/10.

140/1900.

2nd Div.

No. 11 Sanitary Section

Dec 1916

COMMITTEE FOR THE
MEDICAL HISTORY OF THE WAR
Date 31 JAN. 1917

War Diary of
No. 11. Sanitary Section
2nd Division
for December 1916.

Hughes
Capt.

WAR DIARY
or
INTELLIGENCE SUMMARY.
(Erase heading not required.)

Army Form C. 2118.

11 Sanitary Sect.

Hour, Date, Place	Summary of Events and Information	Remarks and references to Appendices
December 1st to 11th	Material for construction work in the men is difficult to obtain. Trucks + ambulances requested + of Rouen, obtained from C.R.E. at the Front had from Guescart and Longvilliers; Estrées-les-Crécy, Brick from Gapennes; Lime from Abbeville. The Railway construction work was completed. At CHATEAU BRAILLY (2nd Div. H.Q.) — one Officers' Latrine, one men's latrine, one large French urinal incinerator. 2. BRAILLY Village — two latrines. At GUESCART — two Officers' Latrines and one men's latrine for the 2nd Div. Gas and Bombing School. At NOYELLES — one men's latrine + ablution bench as a model for the 2nd Div. Officers' School.	

Army Form C. 2118.

WAR DIARY
or
INTELLIGENCE SUMMARY.
(Erase heading not required.)

Instructions regarding War Diaries and Intelligence Summaries are contained in F.S. Regs., Part II. and the Staff Manual respectively. Title pages will be prepared in manuscript.

Hour, Date, Place	Summary of Events and Information	Remarks and references to Appendices
At BERRY	daily inspection of huts. Visit carried out by O.C. Headquarters. The 10 principal wells have now been tested and water found fit for use. About 50 extra huts for men have been prepared by Captain of Headquarters and handed over to the O.C. and a Brigade for troops to walk in whom after instructions have been issued.	
December 11th	Gave a lecture on Sanitation to Medical Officers of No. 5 Field Amb. & 3 to Brigade, at No. 5 Field Amb. at GUEZNCOURT. O.C. Finlay returns on leave to England.	
Dec 12th	Work carried on as usual till Dec. 22nd. date of O.C.'s return. Work carried out unaltered.	

Army Form C. 2118.

WAR DIARY
or
INTELLIGENCE SUMMARY.
(Erase heading not required.)

Hour, Date, Place	Summary of Events and Information	Remarks and references to Appendices
Dec. 23 cd.	Construction of ablution sheds at BRAILLY station too ablution heads made for School at GUEUDECOURT, incinerator built at GUEUDECOURT, 4 seat covered latrine for Police built in BRAILLY, about 200 sanitation boards made for marking wells; manure wells in the area tested & marked; walls cards in Divisional latrines and reported on. Gave lecture on Sanitation at No.100 Field Ambulance. New instructions re sanitary latrines — 5th Army Routine Order No. 283 dated 9.12.16. Brought to my notice. By this new arrangement sanitary sections take over affairs areas and do not move with Division. Great changes involved.	

WAR DIARY
or
INTELLIGENCE SUMMARY.

(Erase heading not required.)

Army Form C. 2118.

Hour, Date, Place	Summary of Events and Information	Remarks and references to Appendices
Dec. 24th	Visited D.D.W.S. 2nd Corps. re new arrangements.	
Dec. 26th	Bathhouse at BRAMLY having completed	
Dec. 27th to 31st	Received instructions from DDWS. 2nd Corps to take over the tracken area GUEUDECOURT — BEAUCOURT — BEAUMETZ — GUEUDECOURT known as the trackea Saulty Area, II Corps, and to choose men now Headquarters on from a position. Made a rapid survey of the area during these days. Also hunted on construction work to higher covered between us by much of practice.	

WAR DIARY
or
INTELLIGENCE SUMMARY.
(Erase heading not required.)

Army Form C. 2118.

Instructions regarding War Diaries and Intelligence Summaries are contained in F.S. Regs., Part II. and the Staff Manual respectively. Title pages will be prepared in manuscript.

Hour, Date, Place	Summary of Events and Information	Remarks and references to Appendices
	No other R.E. material is available to hand Infantry.	
	Summary of Infectious Diseases for December	
	Paratyphoid B. — 1 case	
	Measles — 2 cases	
	Pneumonia — 2 cases	
	Dysentery — 3 cases	
	German Measles — 1 case	
	Scarlet Fever — 1 case	
	Kempt(?) Capt. O.C. No 11 Sanitary Section	

2 DIV

11 SAN SECT

1917 JAN — 1917 MARCH

Box 1011

to 3 ARMY

2nd Division

No. 11 Sanitary Section

140/1917

Jan 1917

COMMITTEE FOR THE
MEDICAL HISTORY OF THE WAR
Date 13 MAR. 1917

WAR DIARY
or
INTELLIGENCE SUMMARY.
(Erase heading not required.)

Army Form C. 2118.

XI Secretary Vol 28

Hour, Date, Place	Summary of Events and Information	Remarks and references to Appendices
BRAILLY. January 1st to Jan. 7th. 1917	Commenced organization of new area — the CONTEVILLE or "Fontein" Landing Area. Chose HQrs at CRAMONT, and fixed up Offices, Mess, workshops, stores. Instructions of the training section; each of 1 Sergeant, 1 other NCO and 1 Private were attached at MAISON PONTHIEU, MAZICOURT, LONGVILLERS and CRAMONT, and areas allotted to them for reconnaissance to that . the whole area was covered. These parties moved out on the 4th and (in instants bitter) in order to commence a complete survey of each sub-area, to	

WAR DIARY
or
INTELLIGENCE SUMMARY.
(Erase heading not required.)

Army Form C. 2118.

Hour, Date, Place	Summary of Events and Information	Remarks and references to Appendices
Jan 8th. Jan 9th. CRAMONT	made sketch maps of each village and plans of all the existing sanitary arrangements. Moved billeting parties from BRAILLY to CRAMONT. Only a small part of the area is occupied by troops at present eg. 5th Inf. Brigade are round MAISON PONTHIEU, R.E. huts are at MIERMONT, and part of 97th Inf. Bde. round CONDRIVILLERS. All the Div. troops moved out latterly having only one Corps troops units in the area. Visited Commanding officers of the area.	
Jan. 10th.	Inspected the Divisional Cavalry (1st Yorkshire Dragoons) at DOMLÉGER and AGENVILLE. Report part 6. D.D.M.S. Inns troops. No report has been made	

Army Form C. 2118.

WAR DIARY
or
INTELLIGENCE SUMMARY.
(Erase heading not required.)

Instructions regarding War Diaries and Intelligence Summaries are contained in F.S. Regs., Part II. and the Staff Manual respectively. Title pages will be prepared in manuscript.

Hour, Date, Place	Summary of Events and Information	Remarks and references to Appendices
Jan 11th	No attempt to deal with its movement which is left through lying & all the stores in the village.	
Jan 12th	Visited MESNIL-DONQUEUR. 18th Division intend the area today.	
Jan 13th	18th Div. left the area today Journey eastward. Visited COURONVILLERS and MAISON ROLAND. Conference of Sanitary Officers at D.D.M.S. II Corps.	
Jan 15th to 19th	51st Division and 61st Division passing through this area very Westwards to their own rest areas. Billets frequently left dirty and latrines with full buckets. 11th Division intend this area to them.	
Jan 20th & 24th	Nothing. The Sanitary Area Supervised by No 11 Sanitary Section	

(73989) W4141—463. 400,000. 9/14. H.&J.Ltd. Forms/C. 2118/10.

WAR DIARY
or
INTELLIGENCE SUMMARY.
(Erase heading not required.)

Army Form C. 2118

Instructions regarding War Diaries and Intelligence Summaries are contained in F. S. Regs., Part II. and the Staff Manual respectively. Title pages will be prepared in manuscript.

Hour, Date, Place	Summary of Events and Information	Remarks and references to Appendices
Jan 21st	Conference practically the whole of the 11th Divn area (3 Inf. Brigades & Artillery) and 1 Brigade men of the 6th Divn.	
Jan 23rd	Chippewa. Inst corps left Corps. IVth Corps took over. Conference of ADMSs & Sanitary Officers at DDMS office IVth Corps.	
Jan 24th	Gave lecture on Sanitation at IVth Corps School at ST. RIQUIER.	
Jan 25th	Another lecture. Above plan	
Jan 26th	Capt. Harriet Rome from Field Amb. C.or Divn. Medical tour for 5c day course in Sanitation. Investigate case of Diphtheria (32nd M.G.C.) at PROUVILLE.	
Jan 27	Visited DOMLEGER. Saw MO of 1st W.Yorks re inspection of Diphtheria contact — the Transport of 32nd M.G.C.	

WAR DIARY
or
INTELLIGENCE SUMMARY.
(Erase heading not required.)

Army Form C. 2118

Instructions regarding War Diaries and Intelligence Summaries are contained in F.S. Regs., Part II. and the Staff Manual respectively. Title pages will be prepared in manuscript.

Hour, Date, Place	Summary of Events and Information	Remarks and references to Appendices
Jan. 27, 28th	Moved field workshops of Ordnance Park from No. 34 to No. 40 Kilo in Crapount. On 27th equipment & men detached 1 personnel of Heavy section in the arcs to fit in with return of power by ADM.S. 11th Div. — New Zealander. — 1 NCO & 1 Private for MAISON PONTHIEU, NEUILLY LE DIEM, ACQUET and ST. LOT. 1 NCO for HALLOYCOURT and BERNATRE 1 NCO for BEAUCOURT, BEAUCOURT 1 Private for MONTIGNY and ST. ACHEUL 1 NCO for CANTELEUX and MERHONT. 1 NCO for PROUVILLE, BEAUMETZ 1 NCO for DOMLEGER and AGENVILLE 1 Private for HEINIL DOMQUEUR and LONGVILLERS 1 NCO for DOMQUEUR LE PLOUY and FRANCE. 1 NCO for HEM Beaufort at DOMQUEUR R. 1 NCO for COULONVILLERS and HAREON ROLLAND 1 Private for CRAMONT, LE FESTEL and MOUCAY Headquarters Organization at CRAMONT.	

Forms/C. 2118/10.
(73989) W4141—463. 400,000. 9/14. H.&J.Ltd.

Army Form C. 2118

WAR DIARY
or
INTELLIGENCE SUMMARY.
(Erase heading not required.)

Instructions regarding War Diaries and Intelligence Summaries are contained in F.S. Regs., Part II. and the Staff Manual respectively. Title pages will be prepared in manuscript.

Hour, Date, Place	Summary of Events and Information	Remarks and references to Appendices
Jan. 29th.	No can yet received from ADT.rs 11th Div. to enable me to get about any news. Went to see him about it, hope information to that end have over arriving to-day: meanwhile these undecided cars which have taken down.	
Jan. 31st.	Conference at D.G.T.rs. Office IV Corps, to meet D.A.D.T.rs (Army). Surprise. One Division in three hours. It a hope that when we go out of the 5th Army, hand on the Sanitary Returns now here to refer the old Divisions.	Kemp/E Capt. O.C. No. 11 Sanitary Section

(73989) W4141—463. 400,000. 9/14. H.&J.Ltd. Forms/C. 2118/10.

140/199 4.

COMMITTEE FOR THE
MEDICAL HISTORY OF THE WAR
Date 4ᵗʰ APR. 1917

2nd Per.

N. Sanitary Sec.

War Diary of
No. 11 Sanitary Section
for February 1917.

Clayton
Capt. OC.

Army Form C.2118
XI Sawthey See

WAR DIARY
or
INTELLIGENCE SUMMARY.
(Erase heading not required.)

Hour, Date, Place	Summary of Events and Information	Remarks and references to Appendices
Feb. 2nd CRAMONT	Received orders by wire from D.H.Q. 5th Army to move to AVELUY to take over from 51st Div. starting return on 3rd inst. This imposible as any personnel or /or Fortress, to wait to arrive personnel on 3rd and leave on 4th.	
Feb. 4th AVELUY	Forced three fatima from CRAMONT to move to AVELUY. Air troubling return.	
Feb. 5th BOUZINCOURT	Moved to BOUZINCOURT as this place is more convenient as a headquarters for my area. New area includes all 2nd Div. area — COURCELETTE, OVILLERS, POZIÈRES, AVELUY, USNA HILL (2nd Div. HQ.), BOUZINCOURT, SENLIS, WARDONVILLE, HÉRISSART, and a large number of this encampments.	

WAR DIARY
or
INTELLIGENCE SUMMARY.
(Erase heading not required.)

Army Form C. 2118

Hour, Date, Place	Summary of Events and Information	Remarks and references to Appendices
Feb. 6th	Weather very cold and trying for men & found in the open. Visited DDM.S. II Corps. Sent out finding parties to each of the following Town Majors. - OVILLERS HUTS, AVELUY, BOUZINCOURT, WARPONVILLE, SENLIS, and HERISSART. The above Town Majors were interviewed with them, Visited ADM.S and Div. and obtained information about this area.	
Feb 7th	Round BOUZINCOURT with Lt Tom Major. Inspected German prisoners Camp. No 32 near BOUZINCOURT.	
Feb. 9th	Conference of Sanitary Officers at DDM.S. Office Toutencourt. Visited Town Major of SENLIS & WARPONVILLE.	
Feb. 10th	Round all BOUZINCOURT with ADMS and Div. Town in a filthy condition. ADMS reported same Inspected Mouquet Camp HQ 2nd Div.	

WAR DIARY
or
INTELLIGENCE SUMMARY.

(Erase heading not required.)

Army Form C. 2118

Hour, Date, Place	Summary of Events and Information	Remarks and references to Appendices
Feb. 11th	Visited Water Points in forward area - OVILLERS POST, OVILLERS HUTS, EIGHT TANKS, BENNET STREET OVILLERS, FRITZ'S WELL OVILLERS, HUN TANK, TULLOCH CORNER, & POZIERES TANK. Reported on pump to A.D.W.S. 2nd Div. and on CROMWELL HUTS Camp to the Town Major.	
Feb. 12th	Inspected SENLIS, HARPONVILLE, & HERISSART, & reported on same to the Town Major.	
Feb. 13th & 14th	Inspected WOLSELEY HUTS, WOLFE HUTS, USNA HILL, and BOUZINCOURT.	
Feb. 16th & 17th	Long carry in camp, wondered for POZIERES & AVELUY.	
Feb. 18th, 19th 20th	Have precautions on Units to use water 19th Dunlop area exhausted to day.	

WAR DIARY
or
INTELLIGENCE SUMMARY.
(Erase heading not required.)

Army Form C. 2118

Hour, Date, Place	Summary of Events and Information	Remarks and references to Appendices
Feb. 20th ALBERT.	Billets parts of ALBERT. Fixed up sanitation in ALBERT with the Townships. Marched into new Headquarters from BOUZINCOURT to ALBERT.	
Jan. 21st.	Cleaned up Office Billets & Stables in ALBERT. Men were in filthy condition.	
Feb. 22nd to 26th.	Employed & reported to R.Ds and Div. on Water supply of three townships, and on horses of Fr.— Latrines at Pozières, and Orders for the use of troops going to and coming from Trenches.	
Feb. 27th	Forwarded complete Monthly Sanitary Report to February to GHQ Army D.M.S.	

W. Hughes
Capt.

140/2043.

2nd Div.

No. 11 Sordon/ Indian

COMMITTEE FOR THE
MEDICAL HISTORY OF THE WAR
Date 11 MAY 1917

XI Saturday

Army Form C. 2118.

WAR DIARY
or
INTELLIGENCE SUMMARY.
(Erase heading not required.)

Hour, Date, Place	Summary of Events and Information	Remarks and references to Appendices
March 1st. ALBERT.	By order of D.D.M.S. Inskip, the villages of WARLOY, CONTAY and VADENCOURT are inclusive in my area. Posts N.C.Os. of Sanitary Sections with the respective Townships.	
March 4th.	New set of dugouts at COURCELETTE to be occupied by Advanced Div. H.Q. were cleansed and disinfected.	
March 6th.	Visited Bde. H.Qs. at COURCELETTE and arranged to send out 1 N.C.O. for Sanitary Supervision of that area — Div. H.Q.s. in dugouts on West Miraumont Road, COURCELETTE and all day out along Artillery Road to POZIERES.	
March 9th.	Two reinforcements arrived in place of Cpl. RUSSELL (Sent to No 29 C.C.S. GEZAINCOURT)	

WAR DIARY
or
INTELLIGENCE SUMMARY.
(Erase heading not required.)

Army Form C. 2118

Instructions regarding War Diaries and Intelligence Summaries are contained in F.S. Regs., Part II. and the Staff Manual respectively. Title pages will be prepared in manuscript.

Hour, Date, Place	Summary of Events and Information	Remarks and references to Appendices
March 9th	and L/Cpl Ford (two which to Umpires & prevented) conference of Umpire Officers at D.H.Q. Estcourt. The provisions of trek oxen, bicores, with 50 h.p. is I fully hopeless ones. At present there are nothing children — they do not belong and seem to the Division, and the Corps & Army equivalents only take a journey start in them. This is shown when gunners must if came to the Eastern or communications for Armies & Reserves.	
March 10th	Visited WARROY and COUNTAY with their respective Townships.	
March 11th	COURCELETTE, POZIERES. There are a large number of camps at present of Infantry divisions in the Third Div. reforming	

WAR DIARY
or
INTELLIGENCE SUMMARY.

(Erase heading not required.)

Army Form C. 2118.

Place	Date	Hour	Summary of Events and Information	Remarks and references to Appendices
	March 12th		Disinfection – Heaters, Groundsheets, Pumps, Dixentin Bowls; Camp (left by British Troops) on N. side of BOUZINCOURT – HEDAUVILLE road; ALBERT Ruelens all inspected	
	March 16th		Gunners return on hospital command.	
	March 17th 12th 18th		Water supplies villages BAPAUME, GRÉVILLERS, BIEFVILLERS: two samples of water from wells and tested them for (a) Amount of Chlorine. (few necessary for Sterilization) (b) Presence Arsenite Cyanide. Many wells found to be broken down or fouled with refuse, but none poisoned. On instructions from 5th Army, I handed over Sanitary supervision of CONTAY, VADENCOURT, WARLOY, etc. to R.D.C.H.V.H.M.E to 36th Sanitary Section	

HEALTH OF R.T. and H.A. R.D. NVILLE

WAR DIARY
or
INTELLIGENCE SUMMARY.

(Erase heading not required.)

Army Form C. 2118.

Place	Date	Hour	Summary of Events and Information	Remarks and references to Appendices
	March 26th		and withdrew my Sanitary men. and Div. left this area 9 my north.	
	March 27th		Monthly Sanitary Report sent to DMS 5th Army — Sanitary cultivation by German prisoners of the huge [movement] of work has now started from La Buissière to Bapaume. Supplies of water (one man and clothing) for the Army they might now pay's in a Casualty scale. 5th Army HQrs. came into Albert. Indian Cavalry Brigade is now in our area for sundry archaeological in winter and summer huts.	
	March 30th		A [Sanitation] Station Barrel to store Hidrations has been completed and fitted up at my Hidration in 91 works [well.] about 170 Furnes carried have been made in the workshop.	

WAR DIARY
or
INTELLIGENCE SUMMARY.

(Erase heading not required.)

Army Form C. 2118.

Place	Date	Hour	Summary of Events and Information	Remarks and references to Appendices
			Of No. 11 Sanitary Section during the month of March, men have been kept out and fresh up throughout the area. The following cases of infectious diseases have been dealt with during the month. Disposed cases	
			German Measles. 41.	
			Measles. 7	
			C.S.M. 3 (including 1 Imperial)	
			Dysentery. 3 (also 2 transported cases)	
			Paratyphoid B. 1	
			Diphtheria. 2 also 1 civilian case	
			Mumps. 4	
			Scarlet Fever. 4	
			Erysipelas. 1	
			Pneumonia. 1	
			Weaylon Capt. O.C. No. 11 Sanitary Section	

2 DIVISION. TROOPS.

100 FIELD AMBULANCE.

1915 NOV TO 1919 JUNE.

11 SANITARY SECTION.

1915 JAN TO 1917 MAR.

1339

2 DIVISION. TROOPS.

100 FIELD AMBULANCE.

1915 NOV TO 1919 JUNE.
11 SANITARY SECTION.
1915 JAN TO 1917 MAR.

www.ingramcontent.com/pod-product-compliance
Lightning Source LLC
Chambersburg PA
CBHW080846010526
44114CB00017B/2380